SANTINI

dal Pescatore

Family Recipes

SANTINI

dal Pescatore
Family Recipes

GIUNTI

Original title:
SANTINI, DAL PESCATORE - RICETTE DI FAMIGLIA

Texts:
Marco Bolasco (preface to the new edition pp. 19-27)
Aldo Santini (preface pp. 31-52)
Antonio Santini (recipes and additional texts pp. 59, 67-231)

Concept, realisation and texts of the recipes:
Nadia with Bruna and Giovanni Santini

Review of the recipes:
Nadia with Bruna and Giovanni Santini

Translation:
Catherine Frost

Layout:
Mario D'Adda

Original photographs, unless otherwise stated (iconografic references in the final pages):
Francesca Brambilla and Serena Serrani

Image processing:
Serena Serrani

Photolithograph:
Nicola Dini

Editorial manager:
Davide Mazzanti

Editing:
Daniela Pincelli

www.piattoforte.it
www.giunti.it

Via Bolognese 165 – 50139 Florence – Italia
Piazza Virgilio 4 – 20123 Milan – Italia
First edition: September 2014

Reprint	Year
5 4 3 2 1 0	2017 2016 2015 2014

FSC
www.fsc.org
MISTO
Carta da fonti gestite in maniera responsabile
FSC® C023532

Printed by Giunti Industrie Grafiche S.p.A. – Prato

To our parents and grandparents; to all the guests who have followed us in our professional evolution; to all the journalists who have visited us, as both food writers and gourmets; to the culinary guides whose ratings have helped to make us known to the world and to bring the world to Runate; to all our collaborators, who offer their professional skills every day; and to all our suppliers who unfailingly procure for us top-quality products.

Contents

Note
*Unless otherwise specified, the ingredients given in the recipes are for four people.

Santini, the Ingredients

The recipe for success of the *Pescatore* at Canneto sull'Oglio, the secret everyone would like to know, lies hidden behind the concept of "apparent simplicity". It is the simplicity of a history, narrated by Aldo Santini in the introduction to this volume, made of up a family and a territory that are fascinating. And of a family that has built, brick by brick, never conspicuously, the identity of a paradigmatic restaurant, one that can serve as ambassador – as no other, perhaps – of *haute cuisine* in the world.

But in this, the restaurant and the family cannot be separated; because in the expert, enthusiastic family management of this beautiful place immersed in the verdant Parco dell'Oglio lies the true secret of the *Pescatore*.

Many years ago, when it seemed nearly impossible to speak of territorial cooking in Italy (*those were the years of culinary exoticism adoring everything foreign, always seeking the new*), here they were celebrating the ritual of a precisely identifiable cuisine, linked by a dual bond to tradition and top-quality products, exalting virtuous domestic skills and practices, those so often buried under sentimental rhetoric that falsifies their true worth. Great Mantuan cuisine, strongly influenced at Canneto by the close vicinity of Cremona and the not far distant Emilia, is a rare ensemble of little culinary jewels, forming part of the collective

unconscious of the "Bassa" and of a shared culture, safeguarded by the local population as a precious heritage. At a time when other restaurants were still afraid to offer authenticity, the Santini family combined tradition with a refined atmosphere, pursuing perfection in the kitchen and warmly welcoming guests in the dining room. They perfected the technique of pasta-making and improved the cooking methods of vegetables. They created tortelli and ravioli that were to form a chapter in the history of Italian cooking. It is no coincidence that the Santini family soon became a beacon for the renewal of many of Northern Italy's great restaurants. Within the range of a few kilometres were some of the noblest tables in Italy, that golden triangle of Mantua, the irresistible destination of all gourmets. A triangle whose apex consisted of the *Pescatore*.

The present enhances the past

Now, some years later, a lot of water has flowed down the Oglio, many things have changed and a few restaurants have closed their doors for good. At Runate, however, the small steps taken have yielded great results and the restaurant has continued to grow. The cuisine – always under matriarchal rule with Bruna and Nadia – now has a new interpreter in Giovanni, able to safeguard the basic commitment to nutritional value, enriching it, thanks to his studies, with a new scientific approach. Without changing gears, everything has been perfected, from sauces to proportions and cooking methods, by cutting down on fats and cooking times for meat and improving the historic recipe for tortelli, because great tradition also depends on minor innovations perfected day by day. And the pasta is not merely romanticism but also, and above all, know-how. Giovanni's low-key innovations have opened the way, through the mists of Mantua, to murmured notes from the Mediterranean, appearing in fragrances and sauces, a skilled interweaving of natural minerals and added herbs. They are also used to flavour a dish without adding salt, to make a familiar recipe – a part of this restaurant's tradition – an ongoing journey; because tradition is not immutable, and with knowledge of the past we can build solid bases for the future. This is how the great classic dishes of Nadia and Grandma Bruna have grown: this too is evolution in "Italianità", little touches where nothing is left to chance.

But the paradigm of a great restaurant is not cooking alone. Here, above all, harmony reigns. The team, increasingly distinguished by the combined work of a family made up of three generations, moves like a well-oiled mechanism. Elegance and sobriety, authenticity with style: a group of musicians performing from Wednesday through Sunday (*Monday and Tuesday are days of rest*), managing its theatre to perfection. A group whose orchestra director, Antonio, is also great when he observes, comforting, proud of his musicians, instilling in them self-confidence and method. It is unusual to find such a successful mingling of generations, with the complementary harmony of different ages, the ability of each to play a role of his own, in a closely interwoven fabric where no one invades the space of a neighbour, whether it be brother, wife or father. It is harmony that the guest perceives when entering this country dining room, as if entering a perfect home. Harmony lies at the basis of each guest's welcome, which is a fundamental part of the restaurant experience at the *Pescatore*. Of this experience, each guest takes home a treasured memory; and it remains the standard for judging any other visit to a great restaurant, a milestone hard indeed to surpass.

The kitchen, then, needs the dining room. And the art and science of service have always found room between these walls, starting from the method for listening attentively to guests. Tradition yes, but mere traditionalism, never. And so the many voyages undertaken by Antonio and Nadia (and now by Alberto, with his tireless curiosity) are the vehicle for discovering the innovations necessary for the implementation of a machine that never stops. It cannot happen here that a dish is forcefully suggested, or that guests feel caught in a piloted experience. Here the server watches, listens, understands, and provides a made-to-order meal in a few minutes. A meal that translates into a succession of dishes, into discovery of the products of this territory, starting from a superb Parmesan cheese, treated here with the dignity it deserves. It is a perfect mix of professional expertise and family, now enhanced by the presence in the dining room of Valentina, Giovanni's wife. And so the serving team moves silently around the guests in this great little country relais: musicians in an orchestra

where an adagio sometimes becomes a rondò. It is rare indeed to hear a guest complain, since desires are often fulfilled even before being expressed.

This is why restauranteurs from all over the world come to the *Pescatore*, swelling the ranks of the guests at the table. To see “how it’s done”, convinced that this is the paradigmatic recipe of great Italian cuisine, which has never been ashamed of its simplicity, fully aware of how valuable it is. Bringing it to the highest level with no need of special effects, without having to mask content by form. But rather by elevating to the maximum the beauty of making and doing, to create an intense, harmonious experience. Because the simplicity, here, is only apparent. It is no coincidence, in fact, that so many – both young chefs and famous maîtres – turn to the *Pescatore* and the Santini family for advice, on what to make and how to do it, in the attempt to do well. But the best way to understand the secret of the *Pescatore*’s success is not to explain it, but to experience it for yourself by coming to Canneto.

Marco Bolasco, July 2014

IMMIGRATION OFFICER
15 APR 2006
HEATHROW (3)
11-08-2009
28.06.02 26
BARCELONA
MEXICO
HONG KONG
GIRIŞ
HIÇBIR
26AUG2
NARITA(1)
JAPANIMMIGRATION
05.77 16
ROISSY-CDG
IMMIGRATION OFFICER
18 JUL 1975
HEATHROW (3)
PRIORITY AIR MAIL
10 1986
SEPTEMBER
SEOUL - LONDON
BERLIN
ARRIVED
12 APR 2007
PERTH AIRPORT
2421
AUSTRALIA
BY AIR MAIL
PAR AVION
PARIS 96
27 -12
25
PRINTEMPS
FURSTENTUM LIECHTENSTEIN
04 NOV. 1998
VADUZ
IMMIGRATION
SERVICE
23SEP 1986
(1441)
HONG KONG
IMMIGRATION
19 APR 1989
SINGAPORE
BANGKOK THAILAND
DEPARTED
18 APR 1989

Travels

Antonio and Nadia Santini's travels are part of the history and development of the restaurant dal Pescatore, *which is deeply linked to Mantua and its territory, but at the same time is the result of comparison and everlasting curiosity towards what was happening to the Italian and European* haute cuisine.

"It was May 9th 1978, at lunchtime, Nadia and I were going to the *Amelia* in Mestre, it was one of our quick outings in search of great dishes. We were on the motorway and the radio programs were interrupted to broadcast the news that the corpse of Aldo Moro, who was killed by the Brigate Rosse, was found in the trunk of a Renault 4 in Via Caetani in Rome. A day that many of us, sadly, will not forget, but for us it was also the day of the fundamental meeting with Franco Colombani."

On that very Tuesday Dino Boscarato, owner of the Venetian restaurant, recommended the meeting, which took place the same evening, with one of the most influential restaurateur in the history of modern Italian cuisine. The trip to Boscarato is just one of the hundreds the Santinis took on their days off when their restaurant, *dal Pescatore* of Canneto sull'Oglio, was closed. The two of them embarked on a passionate research that had them grinding kilometres after kilometres – even 80,000 km a year – in order to meet those who knew how to perform in the kitchens of Italy and France.

"One of my fondest memories is when we took pictures of Giscard d'Estaing, who was being celebrated on the Champs-Elysées – says Antonio – while we were in a bistro devouring fruit from a basket because it was cheap and you could eat the whole content of the basket. I showed him that picture when he came to our restaurant a few years later."

From *Cronache Golose*, by Marco Bolasco and Marco Trabucco,
Slow Food Editore, Bra, 2011.

Grandpa Giovanni explains to Alberto how to make a net (called bertavello) to fish for pike.

"There's no better restaurant, I can assure you"

In Franciacorta, Nadia and Antonio Santini smiled in embarrassment when Paul Bocuse, celebrating his 81st birthday at a table in Maurizio Zanella's restaurant Ca' del Bosco, answered the question of what his favourite restaurant was with the words: "I would like to have the *Pescatore* di Canneto sull'Oglio. There is no better restaurant on the whole planet, I can assure you." Embarrassed and incredulous, Nadia and Antonio, who have made the *Pescatore* their kingdom, thanked Bocuse warmly: "But since you're such a good friend of ours, you have exaggerated", they murmured. He, the world's most famous cook, three Michelin stars since 1965, the first French chef to be awarded the *Légion d'honneur* in 1975.

Then they began to understand the meaning of that exaggeration.

Bocuse, by now the owner of a real empire (restaurants, brasseries, professional cooking schools) recognised *dal Pescatore* as the sanctuary of good cooking, as it was called by Piero Camporesi, offering the cuisine of the "terroir" that he had tasted every day for a week, happily returning whenever he could. In addition to his affectionate admiration for the *Pescatore*, Bocuse considered it a shining example of equilibrium and consistency, a model of the golden mean.

In an age when prize-winning restaurants (*dal Pescatore* has had three Michelin stars since 1996; no other restaurant in Italy has ever stayed at the top for so long) are seduced by requests to open a second place abroad, Nadia and Antonio have always stubbornly refused. They have visited the United States repeatedly, presenting their cuisine at the most illustrious restaurants, but have always said no to America.

They have been to the Far East too, presenting their cuisine again, and have said no to Japan. They have been to Dubai, holding still more demonstrations, and have said no to Dubai.

"We want to stay in Runate" they repeat. Located in the countryside, in the Dell'Oglio Park, the Santini have continuously enlarged their premises. By 2008 they had a staff of eighteen persons and an authorised helicopter pad.

The excellence of *dal Pescatore* has been hailed by John Mariani in "Esquire", a magazine with a circulation of a million and a half, who called it one of "the best restaurants in the world"; and by the "indomitable" American critic, Alan Richman, who in 2007 traversed oceans, countries and continents to dine in the supreme temples of taste, a restaurant every seven thousand kilometres, around the world in seven restaurants. And one of these seven was the *Pescatore*, of which he wrote: "I sampled, among other things, grilled eel, one of the fresh-water fish that Antonio's grandfather cooked in the early 20th century, the way everybody had always cooked them around there for at least five hundred years. At the first bite I thought the dish was a bit too strong. At the last one, I was crazy about it."

Let's ask Antonio, then, a "country gentleman" ("Esquire") tall and robust, a torrent of smiling and likable, a great communicator and tireless promoter of the *Pescatore*'s outstanding qualities, to tell us the story of his grandfather and the eels.

A bridge of boats, the swallows, the flying fish and the Osteria del "Vino e pesce"

"Yes, my grandfather, after whom I'm named, was a gruff, hard man. He knew the Oglio River like the back of his hand. He went fishing there in his boat and became famous on the Oglio as a ferryman. He came from Isola, in the territory of Cremona, not far from here. He fought in World War I. Then, ambitious and stubborn as he was, he rented a bridge of boats and collected toll from all the river traffic: men, animals and vehicles. He knew the lazy, gentle flow of the Oglio in the hot summer months, and its rough force when swollen by the rains coming from Lake Iseo. Later on, going downstream, he met the woman of his life, Teresa Mazzi."

The Mazzi family were farmers at Runate, where they had immigrated. Teresa had been born in Brazil, near São Paolo, where her family worked seasonally on the coffee plantations, taking the place of the slaves who had been freed in the late 19th century. Her brother Paolo instead had been born in Luxembourg.

Today Antonio's wife, "the best woman chef in the world" as she has been called by the French weekly "Le Point", a delightful, cultured woman, recalls the Mazzi family in a poetic expression: "They were like swallows".

The members of the Mazzi family took ship at Genoa and sailed to Brazil for the coffee bean harvest. Then they came back;

long-distance commuters. In the chronicles of Italian labour, this is a little-known chapter.

But Teresa gave up travelling for love. No more Brazil. Grandfather Antonio took her as his bride in 1926. And at Runate, with the *sghei* (money) from the fishing and the coffee they bought the *Pescatore* house, next door to the Mazzi family.

The *Pescatore* house was little more than a shed built of marsh reeds held together with a few bricks, beside a little lake. This was the origin of the future 3-star restaurant. Its signboard read "Vino e Pesce", wine and fish; an "osteria", a tavern, with Teresa in the kitchen and Antonio serving the tables. And since the osteria worked mainly on Sundays, Antonio still had time to fish and sell some of the fish at Piadena to balance the budget. In 1927 Giovanni was born.

It is Giovanni, now an elderly man with white hair, who tells me about his father during my first visit to the *Pescatore*:

"He taught me everything there was to know. The river had no more secrets for me. I went fishing mostly at night and was never afraid. To catch eels, you have to fish at night. A line with a weight and worms attached to it. The eels bite, you just pull them up and that's that. River fishing is an art. You have to know how to steer the boat swept away by the current, and how to mend the nets and know all the tricks and techniques, including the oldest one of the flying fish."

Flying fish?

"They are tiny fish. You catch them in August, using a circular net with floats that you pull up a little at a time until it closes, trapping them inside. You have to walk lightly on the sandy river bank because if they sense the danger they jump out of the water, escape the net and that's the last you ever see of them."

Fishermen, ferry-boat pilots, tavern-keepers, immigrants and even wine-makers. My friend Antonio continues: "They bought grapes in the territory of Mantua. Grandpa knew how to make wine too; and what wine! His Lambrusco was really strong, as much as ten and a half degrees. But when the war broke out and my father Giovanni was only thirteen, things looked really bad. Grandpa was drafted into the army at Cremona, even though he was 42 years old and had already fought bravely in World War I. Here everything seemed to collapse. It all fell onto the shoulders of Grandma Teresa. There was no more Lambrusco. It was a disaster. While Grandpa was on leave he took the chance to go to Carpi and buy it; no longer the grapes, but Lambrusco already made into wine and bottled. He had to cross the Po on a barge. Once there was a hail of machine gun fire, that shot holes in all the wine-barrels."

And here at Runate, how did you manage during the war? By fishing?

"That's right. My father Giovanni went fishing on the Oglio even at night, and since he caught more fish than we could eat, he sold some of them in the nearby villages."

After the tragic years of war, peace finally came and the country began to rebuild. Grandpa Antonio returned to his place beside Teresa. The little restaurant had survived the crisis and Giovanni had grown up quickly. The signboard "Vino e Pesce" began to attract people again.

My friend Antonio continues:

"My grandparents built up a clientele again. People came from as far away as Cremona, on bicycles. There was little or no traffic. The only thing you had to be careful of were the potholes in the dirt roads. At our place it was the usual menu, fried fish, Lambrusco, and games of *bocce*. Grandma Teresa cooked stewed eels with peas. And pike with a white sauce. Today, as then, we use raw materials from our own territory, if not from our own farmyard, fishpond and vegetable garden. At the most we buy some seasonal things at the market in Canneto. We don't have oysters around here, but you will find them on our menu among the appetisers. I have to have something to make the foreigners feel at home, and to impress the snobs. I can't ignore salt-water fish, of course. I can get it really fresh in Cremona. And the last time you came here and we served you chicken livers, that chicken had been scratching around in the orchard a couple of hours before; understand?'

I understand perfectly. Your cuisine is of the "terroir", as the French say.

"Call it what you like, 'terroir' sounds convincing. My grandmother Teresa didn't speak French but Brazilian, the Portuguese language.

Dal Pescatore
Santini

Giovanni Santini and Bruna: linen tablecloths, a big kitchen and Gianni Brera on Sundays

"Grandpa Antonio would never have imagined that his grandson would replace Lambrusco with Sassicaia and Masseto. I take my hat off to the vines from your Province of Livorno: Barbaresco di Gaja, the spumante Ca' del Bosco, and the Pergole Torte of our Sergio Manetti from Radda in Chianti, may the god of wine bless him. Do you remember the fabulous dinners we had down there at Montevertine? In his dream house, around the hearth with its blazing fire and the vitrines of Riedel glasses, a hundred or so of every shape. Sergio played the glasses by striking them lightly against each other, giving concerts that would be the envy of Abbado and the Berlin Philharmonic."

And how could forget? I miss Sergio, more than I can say.

"My cellar contains the finest wines of Europe and America, without forgetting South Africa and Australia. To stay at the top, you have to keep on this level. All I've done is follow the teachings of my father and grandfather. I have remained a Santini dell'Oglio who has adapted to his own day, and with more ambition than they had. Maybe too much. But if I had any less, we wouldn't have as much fun, Nadia and I."

It is just because you are having fun that your clients breathe an air here that is unlike that of any other top restaurant.

But let's get back to the postwar period. At "Vino e Pesce", in ad dition to the fried fish, the eels and the pike, didn't you begin to serve first courses with home-made pasta at that time? And isn't it your specialty today? Made with fresh eggs and with the value added by Nadia, who uses thirty egg yolks without the whites for every kilo of pasta?

In the meantime, Giovanni got married in 1952. His bride was Bruna Rubes, born in 1929, the daughter of farmers from Asola, not far from Runate. And in 1953 Antonio was born, on April 19. Bruna entered the kitchen working alongside Teresa and bringing the experience of her own family. Now "Vino e Pesce" deserved to be called a trattoria, not just an osteria.

Linen tablecloths. A more extensive menu. And a clientele coming also from the city. One of the first illustrious guests was Aldo Cortina, the Milanese bookseller, future publisher and art gallery owner. And then Gianni Brera, the number one sportswriter, arrived. A hearty, argumentative Lombard, Brera made us all feel like Lombards. Giovanni explains, "What gave us satisfaction was the fact that the people who came once, came back again. Brera came almost every Sunday, inspiring us to get better and better."

Antonio enters the conversation: "In the meantime we had spread out. For ten thousand lire I bought the house with the land around it, four hectares of woodland and marshes. My father started going to Cremona and Mantua on a Lambretta scooter, no longer by bicycle. In one of my childhood memories, a bunch of students from Brescia who were going to Parma on Vespas to attend the Faculty of Medicine stopped at our place. And then on their way back home they stopped here again. Some of them kept on coming even after they had graduated. And I can tell you still more: in my restaurant I have clients from around Brescia, now distinguished professionals, who tell me how when they were young they all used to say how good the salami was in my father's trattoria. I tell them we still have our own salami, and it's still just as good. They sample a slice and say, "Yes, it's really good, but that was something else. It had a different flavour."

Of course it did. It had the flavour of their youth.

The students' train, back and forth: Antonio and Nadia enter the scene

But let's talk about you and Nadia. How did you meet? Was Nadia born on the Oglio too?

"No, I'm from the Veneto region, the Province of Vicenza."

She seems clear about making this distinction.

Nadia is calm, polite and always speaks in a low voice. And she is very affectionate with her good friends, as I well know, but behind her gentle aspect you can feel the determination and a moral rectitude that makes her an iron woman.

To anyone who calls the Santini a patriarchal family, Antonio exclaims, "Patriarchal? But this is a matriarchy!" And in fact, the three women of the three generations of Santini, first Teresa, then Bruna with Teresa, and today Nadia with Bruna, have been crucially important to the success of the three Santini men.

From around Vicenza? Where, exactly?

"From San Pietro Mussolino, in the Chiampo Valley. It's situated at 300 meters above sea level, but where we lived it was a lot higher, and we went down to San Pietro to go to Mass on Sunday. My earliest memory takes me back up there, to the little house built of stone where I was born. I remember the geese, looking enormous to me as a child, that cackled along the rows of grape vines. I remember the road that led to the river, the Chiampo. I had my own river, and its water was crystal clear, flowing over the rocks, real drinking water. I remember very well the road lined with cherry trees where I ran after the big geese with a little stick in my hand."

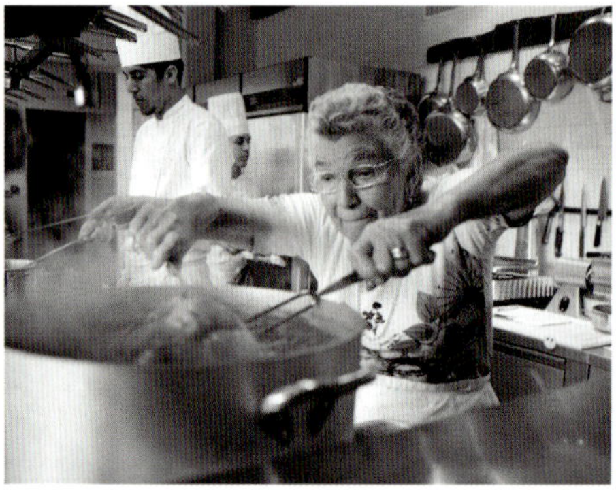

Who would ever have thought that one day you would be crowned the best woman chef in the world?

"It's a title that haunts me. I'm no better than lots of others. It's working together with Bruna and all our assistants in the kitchen, starting with my son Giovanni who takes care of the first courses and the desserts, with the commitment that Antonio and I assumed even while having fun, as he rightly says, because if not it would have been too hard; it is this teamwork with a strong sense of direction, in a place we are continuing to improve, it's all this that makes *dal Pescatore* a very special restaurant."

And how did you and Antonio meet?

"First on the high-school students' train from Piadena to Mantua and then on the one the university students take, from Piadena to Milan. We were both enrolled in the Faculty of Political Science, at the State University."

Antonio continues, "I was the first member of the Santini family to go to university. My parents thought this was a big change and that their only son would surely be taking another road in life. What should they do? They were beginning to feel tired. 'We're glad you're going to have a college degree', my father said, 'Now I want to go everywhere and see everything and we'll do something easier.' But I really didn't want to give up Runate. And in agreement with Nadia we decided to carry on my family's work. In our own way. No more college degree. We were married on May 6, 1974."

Nadia speaks up:

"During our long honeymoon in France we tried to decide what kind of restaurant we were going to create, what innovations we should introduce. Every evening we looked for a new experience in some temple of fine cuisine. We came home with the awareness that what guests ask of the table is perfection, emotion and most of all character. Everything must speak to them of our own territory. We were convinced that you should never copy anything. The most important thing for us is having had behind us a family with a wealth of experience in this field, a family that supported us."

The circle closes, *dal Pescatore* is born: a vast horizon and healthy roots

Giovanni and Bruna, the second-generation Santini, set aside their pride and principles. They knew that the third generation, their son Antonio and his young wife, had the right to change. They were ready to accompany them, offering both moral and financial assistance. And so the restaurant *dal Pescatore* was born, with Nadia and Bruna in the kitchen demonstrating the crucial importance of culture, a willingness to compare their cuisine with others and to learn from all while imitating none.

You were already among those in favour of territorial cuisine. You had the good example of Franco Colombani, whose own master had been Peppino Cantarelli.

Antonio: "My first time at Colombani's restaurant, *Il Sole* di Maleo, was one evening in May 1978. The restaurant's clientele came from the world of publishing and show business. The gourmets met at Maleo to experience real emotions. We were greeted with fraternal cordiality. Then they came to see us and gave us the right advice.

You know how he was. One day we happened to find ourselves at his place, and Franco said, "I found reservations for two Santini. I thought there must have been some mistake."

Colombani himself had received advice at Samboseto from Peppino Cantarelli and his wife Mirella, a great chef, while returning by Vespa from Pisa where was studying engineering.

The Bertolucci from Parma, father and son, the poet and the filmmaker, greatly appreciated him. The actors and technicians who worked on the film "Novecento", shot around that area, discovered the delicacies of real Italian cooking at Cantarelli's place.

Antonio: "The last time Franco Colombani came to see us, before leaving us in such a dramatic way, he embraced us and exclaimed, "I'm as happy for your three stars as if I had won them myself!"

Three stars and two wonderful youngsters: Antonio and Nadia look to the future

Antonio and Nadia have two children, two boys. In the Runate matriarchy, only sons are born. How could three iron ladies like Teresa, Bruna and Nadia give birth to girl babies? Their first child, Giovanni, was born in 1976 and the second, Alberto, in 1983. They have always appreciated the work of their parents and grandparents; even while going to school, they entered the world of the *Pescatore*.

"When I was little", says Giovanni, "I dried the glasses standing on a stool so I could reach the counter."

After high school Giovanni enrolled in the School of Culinary Science and Technology. He graduated in 2004 with Valentina, his girlfriend (*their wedding took place in 2011, Ed.*). And Valentina too, with Giovanni, now forms part of the brigade.

Alberto, who is studying Economy at Parma (*he graduated in 2009, Ed.*), is interested in hospitality and assists his father in the dining room. And so the fourth generation of Santini is already at work.

Dal Pescatore has a great future before it, to the good fortune of Antonio and Nadia who, still young, continue to enjoy their glorious achievements. Giovanni, Alberto and Valentina were thrilled when the restaurant won the highest recognition. And when their parents were invited to the United States and Japan to demonstrate their supreme skill. When Bocuse, to celebrate his wedding anniversary, came to dine at the *Pescatore*. When other famous chefs also came to the *Pescatore*: Troisgros, Ducasse, Veyrat, Blanc, Haeberlin, Westermann, Vergé, Chibois, Bras, Wynants and then Rollinger, Finkbeiner, Maccioni and, as time went on, all of the great names. When Carlo Azeglio Ciampi, as President of the Republic, stated that the identity of a people, and thus its culinary traditions, are a heritage to be intelligently protected. When in March 2006, to celebrate

the fifty years of the Michelin, their mother left the imprint of her hands in the terracotta of the mould at the Accademia Barilla in Parma. When *dal Pescatore* received the award "Cavalieri della grande cucina italiana" (Knights of great Italian cuisine). When in London, in March of 2008, Nadia and Antonio were named ambassadors of Italian taste, and Nadia was the first woman to be included in the list of the world's best chefs, a confirmation of the opinion expressed by a French periodical, "Nadia is the best woman chef in the world".

All of these episodes fill the fourth-generation Santini with pride, convincing them to continue the marvellous adventure of the *Pescatore*.

Aldo Santini, 2008

Pumpkin Tortelli: analysis and comment on a traditional recipe

Tortelli filled with pumpkin is the most emblematical and representative dish in the cuisine of Mantua and its territory. We might be able to imagine Mantua without its lakes and its castle, but not without a dinner on Christmas Eve, a so-called "fast day", with pumpkin tortelli. The origin of this dish has been lost in the history of cooking, leaving no trace. What has been handed down is, in fact, not the pure recipe, but a particular flavour and the memory of "how grandma used to make it"; in this sense, the memory of taste is irreplaceable. Each family safeguards the secret of the filling as a heritage of originality and a sign of recognition. It is the families that hand down culinary secrets over the years, and spread them throughout the territory.

The sweetish taste of pumpkin is generally appreciated by people accustomed to contrasting tastes (sweet-and-savoury, sweet-and-sour). In the case of these tortelli, many flavours are combined: the sweet taste of pumpkin mingles with the salty flavour of Parmesan cheese, the slightly bitter tang of amaretti and the sharp bite of mustard, while nutmeg introduces an oriental note. Pumpkin tortelli, then, is a dish that calls for psychological preparation. And you will never taste two dishes of tortelli exactly the same, even at a short distance, in going from house to house or from town to town. Traditionally, they are dressed only with melted butter and grated Parmesan; and this is the best way to taste the filling, to enhance its flavour to the highest. But let's make the pumpkin tortelli speak for themselves, in a poem in dialect that is a hymn to their excellence:

Suca al foran da cla bona
e mostarda da Cremona,
amaret e pan gratà,
dal formai in quantità;
on per d'of, dla nòs moscata...
tut sta roba ben misiada
On bel sfòi e ben tirà
ti t'avrè za preparà.

Sora l'ass dle taiadele
taìa, intant, le to pastelle,
e col pist gh'è in dla supera
sensa poesia, con manera,
impinisle pian, bel bel,
dagh la forma d'on capel...

[Berni, 1955]

2000

DIETARY ELEMENTS PER PORTION OF PUMPKIN TORTELLI (ANALYSIS)

HUMIDITY

tare	wt	after stewing	% humidity	dry substances
12	93,1	48,6	60,69	39,31

PROTEINS

wt sample	% protein	mean
0,9557	3,096	3,14
0,9901	3,187	

FATS WITH HYDROLYSIS

tare	wt	after stewing	% lipids mean
0	0	0	0

STARCH

wt sample	reading	% starch
2,5	0,8	8,6956522

SUGARS

wt sample	ml thiosulfate	% sugars
2,5	17,8	70,72

A dish of pumpkin-filled tortelli is well-balanced in nutrients, with the advantage of containing a food, pumpkin, which rarely appears on our tables. A member of the cucurbitacea family, pumpkin is low in fats and sugar, appreciated by dieticians for its low caloric content.

In our case, however, the amount of fat in the dish is increased by the butter and Parmesan dressing; as concerns the sugar content, note that the recipe for the filling (amaretti, mustard and breadcrumbs) significantly increases the carbohydrate level. Like other orange-coloured foods, pumpkin is especially rich in vitamin A (good for the formation of epithelial tissue and the renewal of cells) and potassium (indispensable for the transmission of nerve impulses, the synthesis of some enzymes and, in combination with sodium, for the hydric equilibrium of the cells).

According to the National Nutrition Institute, 200 grams of pumpkin a day are enough to cover the mean daily requirement of our organism. To its many virtues, the humble pumpkin adds one that most people are probably unaware of: that of being a "biologically correct" product. Easily grown on qualitatively poor land, it has no need of chemical fertilisers. Furthermore, if attacked by parasites, it can be "cured" with the traditional products used in organic farming – such as sulphur – instead of modern insecticides.

And this is news that, if better known, could favour the consumption of pumpkin beyond all expectations.

Giovanni Santini

A Chorus of Menus

Black truffle soup

Paul Bocuse

A dish created for the Élysée Palace on the occasion of the awarding of the Legion d'honneur to Paul Bocuse by the President Valéry Giscard d'Estaing on February 25, 1975

Ingredients (serves 1)

- Vermouth (Noilly Prat) 1 tablespoon
- Truffle water 1 tablespoon
- Double beef consommé 1 cup
- Black truffles 1 oz
- Foie gras 2 teaspoons
- Carrots, onions, celery and champignon mushrooms in equal parts, chopped fine and sautéd in butter 2 teaspoons
- Boiled beef (shoulder) diced in cubes 1/4" per side 1 oz
- Sea salt and freshly ground black pepper
- A round of puff pastry 2 oz
- Egg yolks to gloss

Spread the garnish over the bottom of a soup tureen: the vegetables, the diced beef, the foie gras broken into pieces and the finely sliced truffles.

Add the vermouth, truffle water and consommé.

Cover the soup tureen with the round of puff pastry, pressing it down around the edges to seal it and keep all of the fragrance of the soup inside the tureen.

Brush the top with the beaten egg yolk. Bake in a preheated oven at 425 °F for 18-20 minutes, then remove from the oven and serve.

Much more than a recipe, this dish dedicated by the great Bocuse to the President of the Republic Valéry Giscard d'Estaing has strong symbolic meaning. It is, in fact, the clearest testimonial to the tribute rendered by the French politician to haut cuisine, acknowledged to play a primary role in promoting the image of France the world over.

In the glass: suggested wines

To accompany this dish, the sommelier Mathieu Vial recommends two great wines: Château Pétrus 1975 Pomerol (Bordeaux, France); Châteauneuf du Pape 1976 (Côte du Rhône, France).

We are proud to offer you three sublime recipes, the precious gift of three great families we are honoured to call our friends. Paul Bocuse and his wife Raymonde; Paul, Jean Pierre and Marc Haeberlin; Jean, Pierre, Michel and Marie Pierre Troisgros really have no need of presentations. They are simply unique, with their inexhaustible creativity that has given rise over the years to a real revolution in the culinary world and a whole universe of wholly inimitable dishes.

Their restaurants are the only ones to have had three prestigious Michelin stars for over forty years. Without interruption. Such success can only come from a combination of different ingredients. It is a perfect recipe based on a simple postulate: research, synthesis, simplicity, and top-quality products.

To do our work, in fact, technical capability and a good dose of genius are not enough alone. The common ground of their and our concept of cuisine is the curiosity that seeks to know and understand, the same curiosity that sends us travelling on the hunt for new ideas, intercepting the rapid changes of our time, seeking encounters and confrontation with our brilliant colleagues. Without ever forgetting our own experience, and always putting to good use our love for the products of our own territory. Our friends' style, like our own, is based on a long family tradition, from where each of them started out toward new horizons. Just as we did.

It has always fallen to young people to introduce innovations. In our family, it was once our grandparents, then our parents, then Nadia and I who brought in new ideas; and today it is Alberto, Giovanni and Valentina.

Antonio Santini

Sardines, a touch of kaiseki

Michel Troisgros

Ingredients (serves 4)

- Sardines 12
- Caramelised onions 6
- Fresh sea fennel 3 1/3 tablespoons
- Lemon 1
- Fleur de sel
- Olive oil
- Yuzu Kosho (hot red pepper paste with rind of yuzu, a citrus fruit similar to the clementine) 1 teaspoon
- Salt

FOR THE MARINADE
- White wine 2 cups
- Mineral water 2 cups
- Pepper 1/2 teaspoons
- Sugar 2 tablespoons
- Rock salt 1 1/2 teaspoons
- Cinnamon 1/4 stick
- White wine vinegar 1/3 cup
- Onions 2
- Carrots 5
- Gelatine 8 leaves

FOR THE CARAMELISED ONIONS
- Small white onions 1/4 lb
- White vinegar 2/3 cup
- Acacia honey 1/2 cup
- Sugar 1/2 cup
- Mineral water 1/2 cup
- Bay leaves 4

For the marinade: in a pot, mix the white wine, vinegar, sliced onions and carrots, the mignonette pepper, sugar, rock salt and cinnamon stick. Simmer for 30 minutes, then remove from the heat and leave to steep for an hour.

Strain the broth through a cloth and taste it for seasoning. Put it back on the stove and stir in the leaves of gelatine. Pour the broth into a mould lined with oven paper, forming a layer 1/4" thick, and let the gelatine cool and set.

Prepare the caramelised onions according to the recipe.

Remove the heads from the sardines, clean and carefully fillet them. Salt them on the flesh side and spread them with a little Yuzu Kosho.

Remove the leaves from the sea fennel. Rinse it well, then plunge it briefly into boiling water, removing while still crunchy. Cool in ice water to keep it green.

Remove the gelatine from the mould. Cut it into 12 squares 2 1/2 inches per side. Place a filleted sardine at the centre of each gelatine square. Close it delicately like a book, then trim the edges evenly.

Place 4 sardine fillets on each plate. Surround with petals of caramelised onion and sea fennel. Dribble with lemon juice and olive oil and sprinkle with fleur de sel.

For the caramelised onions: use small onions of the same size. Peel the onions and plunge them into a pot of boiling water for 3 minutes, removing them with a skimmer. Place the onions in a jar or a plastic box.

Melt the sugar in a saucepan. When it turns light caramel in colour, add the lukewarm water and bring to a boil. Add the bay leaves, honey and vinegar. Bring back to a boil, add the onions and place in the refrigerator.

In the glass: suggested wines

To accompany this dish, the sommeliers Jean-Jacques Banchet and Christian Vermorel suggest: Menetou-Salon 2006 – Minchin (Loire, France); Pouilly-Fuissé 2004 "Tradition"– Dom. Valette (Bourgogne, France).

Frog-leg mousseline Paul Haeberlin

Marc Haeberlin

Ingredients (serves 6)

- Frog legs 4 1/2 lb
- Filleted pike 1/2 lb
- Egg whites 2
- Cream 2 cups
- Butter 2/3 cup
- Riesling 1/2 bottle
- Shallots 4
- Spinach 1 lb
- Clove of garlic 1
- Roux 1 tablespoon
- Lemon 1/2
- Salt and pepper
- Chives

To cook the frog legs: in a wide pan, wilt the finely-chopped shallots with the butter; add half of the frog legs, the Riesling, salt and pepper. Cover and simmer for 10 minutes. When done, strain the frog legs. Strain the pan juices and scrapings through a chinois and return to the pan, simmering to reduce the amount by half.

To prepare the mousse: debone the remaining frog legs raw. Using a fine mincer, mince the flesh of the pike and the frog legs. Place the meat in the blender, adding the egg whites. Blend, adding an equal amount of cream a little at a time; salt and pepper. When the mousse is smooth and even, pour it into a terrine.

For the spinach: blanch the spinach in salted boiling water, simmering for 5 minutes. Drain it in a strainer and squeeze it well with the hands to remove all of the water. In a sauteuse pan, place 3 1/3 tablespoons of butter and the peeled clove of garlic. When the butter begins to foam, add the spinach, salt and pepper, and heat for 5 minutes.

Debone the cooked frog legs and set the meat aside.

Butter 8 soufflé dishes. Using a round-mouthed pastry bag, line the sides of the soufflé dishes with the mousse. Fill the hollow with the cooked frog legs and cover with a layer of filling.

Place the soufflé dishes in a wide shallow pan half full of water and bake them for 15 minutes.

To prepare the sauce: bind the reduced pan juices with the roux and bring to a boil. Add the cream and whip the sauce with the rest of the butter, diced and kept very cold. Finish with the lemon juice, add salt and pepper to taste.

Turn the soufflé dishes out onto a serving dish garnished with spinach. Drizzle the sauce over the mousseline and sprinkle with finely chopped chives.

In the glass: suggested wines

The sommelier Serge Dubs recommends: Riesling Schlossberg Grand Cru 2005 – C. Faller et Filles, Kaysersberg (Alsace, France); Riesling Kastelberg Grand Cru 2005 – R. Gresser, Andlau (Alsace, France).

Recipes

Hors d'oeuvres

A DINNER AT THE RESTAURANT can begin with hors d'oeuvres, followed by a first course, a second course and then a dessert, because when we want to eat something special, each dish contributes to the harmony of the meal. In presenting the hors d'oeuvres, then, we should proceed logically, taking into account "what comes afterward". Hors d'oeuvres should be light and delicate in taste, without overpowering flavours or overly strong sauces. When a menu has been skilfully combined, food can become happiness, emotion and the fount of wellbeing. Even at the darkest moments in history, human beings always been concerned with preparing food to ensure their survival; but cooking is much more than a necessity of life. It is the place of human encounter par excellence, it is something to be handed down from generation to generation, it conveys our taste, reflects our character, mentality, and attitudes. It is our heritage and our identity.

Zucchini and mint compote

Ingredients (serves 4 -6)

4 fresh long zucchini about 5 oz. each
Shallot 1
Green celery 1 stalk
Extra-virgin olive oil 3 tablespoons
Vegetable stock 3/4 cup
Granulated gelatine 3/4 teaspoon
Mint leaves
Basil sauce 1 tablespoon
Salt

FOR THE BASIL SAUCE
Basil leaves 20
Extra-virgin olive oil

Extra-virgin olive oil
Traditional balsamic vinegar

Time: **20'**
plus chilling time

Preparation

1. For the sauce, simmer the basil leaves for 2 minutes, cool them in iced water, drain them and blend in the blender with extra-virgin olive oil.

2. Sauté in oil a mixture of chopped shallot and chopped celery, then add the sliced zucchini. Salt, add a little stock and continue to simmer over moderate heat until the liquid has almost entirely evaporated.

3. Add the gelatine, diluted in half a ladle of hot stock, the basil sauce and the mint leaves torn into bits; pour the mixture into a mould. Refrigerate for at least 8 hours.

4. Serve the compote cut into slices and dribbled with extra-virgin olive oil and a few drops of traditional balsamic vinegar.

In the glass: suggested wines

Sauvignon Vette di San Leonardo – Guerrieri Gonzaga Tenuta di San Leonardo (Trentino-Alto Adige); Sauvignon – Brandolini d'Adda (Friuli); Bougogne Blanc – Coche Dury (Champagne, France); Jacques Selosse Initial Blanc de Blancs Grand Cru (Champagne, France); Chardonnay – Planeta (Sicily).

Porcini with rosemary flavoured calf liver

Ingredients

Calf liver 16 small cubes
Fresh porcini mushrooms 2 cups
Garlic 1 whole clove
Fresh onion 1/2 sliced fine
Butter 1/2 cup
Breadcrumbs
Rosemary and sage
Salt

Time: **10'**

Preparation

1. Clean the mushrooms thoroughly and slice them.

2. In a non-stick pan, heat 1/4 cup of butter, a twig of rosemary and the garlic. Add the porcini only when the butter begins to sizzle. Stir constantly to keep them crunchy and tasty.

3. In the meantime, coat the cubes of liver with the breadcrumbs and brown them in a pan with the rest of the butter, twigs of rosemary and sage leaves, until they develop a golden-brown crust.

4. Arrange the cubes of liver and the mushrooms at the centre of a platter and decorate with green salad and rounds of fresh onion.

In the glass: suggested wines

San Leonardo – Guerrieri Gonzaga Tenuta di San Leonardo (Trentino-Alto Adige); I Sodi di San Nicolo – Castellare (Tuscany); La Querciola – Massavecchia (Tuscany); Pergole Torte – Montevertine (Tuscany); Valpolicella – Quintarelli (Veneto)

Oysters in gelée

Ingredients

Oysters, Belon or other kinds at your discretion (buy from a top-quality fish-shop that will give you oysters already washed and well opened) 24/30
Venus clams 24/30 opened

FOR THE GELATINE
Water 2/3 cup
Franciacorta or Trento DOC 2/3 cup
Granulated gelatine 1 tablespoon
Fresh red watermelon 1 wedge
Green celery 1 small stalk

Time: 30'

Preparation

1. If you open the shellfish yourself, be careful to leave the flesh in the concave part. Place the opened shellfish on cracked ice to keep cold.

2. For the gelatine, bring the water flavoured with chopped celery to the boil, then add the granulated gelatine. Strain and let cool until luke-warm.

3. Add the Franciacorta to this liquid and pour the gelatin over the oysters and Venus clams. After about 10 minutes, when it begins to solidify, serve with slices of watermelon.

In the glass: suggested wines

Cuvée Annamaria Clementi Rosé – Ca' del Bosco (Lombardy); Bellavista Franciacorta Riserva - Vittorio Moretti (Lombardy); Champagne Dom Ruinart Rosè – Ruinart (France); Champagne Grand Cru Blanc de Blancs – Steinbrück (France);

Artichokes and Calf Liver with Butter and Rosemary

Ingredients

Artichoke hearts 4
Butter 2 oz
Rosemary 1 twig
Calf liver 1/2 lb
Green onion
(or small onion) 2-3 slices
Breadcrumbs
Salt and pepper

Time: around **10'**

Preparation

1. Slice the artichoke hearts very fine and place them in a copper pan with the hot butter and a twig of rosemary; salt, pepper, and sauté gently over very low heat.

2. Remove the artichokes from the pan and keep them warm.

3. Cut the calves' liver into 3/4" cubes, roll them lightly in breadcrumbs and place them, along with a few slices of green onion, back in the same pan the artichokes were cooked in; salt and pepper.

4. Mix the artichokes and liver together and serve piping hot.

Calf liver, which must always be very fresh and of the highest quality, is excellent combined with porcini sautéd in butter. This variation, like the recipe given here, is a one of the Pescatore's classic dishes.

In the glass: suggested wines

Since we serve this dish as an hors d'oeuvre at the Pescatore, we usually accompany it with a white wine or a red one with a good degree of acidity. Among the whites, we advise: Friuli Isonzo Chardonnay – Vie di Romans (Friuli Venezia Giulia); Alteni di Brassica – Gaja (Piemonte); Le Vignole – Colle Picchioni (Lazio). Among the reds instead, a Pinero – Ca' del Bosco (Lombardy) or a Refolà Vigne di San Pietro – C. Nerozzi (Veneto).

dal Pescatore

Lobster in gelée de Champagne with Ossetra Royal caviar, Tuscan extra-virgin olive oil and ginger root

Ingredients (serves 6)

Live lobsters 3
Leafy herbs to line the terrine
Tuscan extra-virgin olive oil 4 full tablespoons
Ossetra caviar 6 teaspoons
Marinated ginger root 20 slices

FOR THE GELATINE
Vegetable stock 1 ladle
Small green celery 1 stalk
Vegetable gelatine 1/4 oz
Champagne 1/2 cup

FOR THE MARINATED GINGER ROOT
Ginger 1 root
White wine to cover 2 1/2 cups
White wine for the marinade 1/2 cup
Vinegar for the marinade 1/2 cup
Sugar

Lemon juice a few drops
Tuscan extra-virgin olive oil

Preparation

1. Wash the herbs and remove the leaves from the stems, cutting them off with sharp scissors; bundle the leaves together and plunge them into boiling water for one minute. Cool them in water with ice (or cold water). Carefully line the whole terrine with the herbs, leaf by leaf.

2. Cook the lobsters in boiling water for at least a minute and a half, then plunge them into water with ice to cool.

3. Cut open the lobster tails and claws; arrange the pieces of lobster in the terrine and cover with the last leaves of the herbs.

4. For the gelatine, boil the stock flavoured with the celery, add the vegetable gelatine and let cool. Stir in the Champagne and pour the mixture into the terrine.

5. For the marinated ginger, peel and slice the root; place the slices in a small pot. Cover with 3/4 cup of white wine and bring to the boil. Pour off the wine, which will have become very spicy. Repeat this step 2 or 3 times; cover for the last time with a mixture of white wine and vinegar in equal parts, and a little sugar. Bring to the boil again and serve cold.

6. Place the lobster terrine in a wide pan half-filled with water and bake for 2-3 minutes at 345 °F. Remove from the oven and cool in the refrigerator for about 4 hours. Slice and place each portion on a plate with a teaspoon of caviar and 3-4 slices of marinated ginger root.

7. Finish with a few drops of lemon juice and a light dribbling of Tuscan extra-virgin olive oil.

Time: 30'
plus cooling time

This dish is a variation of the classic Lobster and Salmon Terrine, created in 1990 by the Pescatore. You can find the recipe in our first book, published by Giunti in 2001.

In the glass: suggested wines

With this dish we recommend a sparkling white wine or a Champagne.
Our suggestions are: Franciacorta Annamaria Clementi – Ca' del Bosco (Lombardy); Trento Classico Riserva Giulio Ferrari (Trentino); Moët et Chandon Cuvée Dom Pérignont – Enoteque 1993 (Champagne, France); Cuvée Louise 1998 – Pommery (Champagne, France); Selosse Initiale (Champagne, France).

Petit Gris snails with porcini, aromatic herbs and sweet garlic sprouts

Ingredients

Small snails 80
Butter 1/2 cup
Small onions 2
Green celery 1 stalk
Small carrot 1
Fresh parsley 1 bunch
Beef or vegetable stock 2 1/2 ladles
Water 1 ladle
Garlic (with its sprouts) 2 cloves
Cornmeal
Rosemary 1 twig
Porcini mushrooms, medium size 1
Salt

Time: **1h**

Preparation

1. Drop the snails into boiling water and simmer for 20 minutes. Drain and rinse them under cold water. Using a fork, remove the snails from their shells, eliminating the black curl at the end.

2. Sprinkle the snails with cornmeal and salt to remove any viscosity, then wash them in abundant cold water.

3. Place 2 tablespoons of butter in an aluminium pan and melt over medium heat. Sauté for a few minutes the finely chopped onions, 1/2 stalk of celery and carrot, then add 1 1/2 cloves of garlic and the snails.

4. Cover with 2 ladles of stock and water. Simmer for at least 10-15 minutes.

5. Meanwhile, in another aluminium skillet, sauté the rest of the celery and a few slices of onion with 1/2 ladle of stock. When the mixture reaches boiling point, add the parsley leaves, 1/2 clove of garlic and 2 tablespoons of butter cut directly from the stick.

6. Pour these ingredients into a blender pitcher, blend well and strain through a fine strainer. The cream of parsley prepared in this way goes very well with snails.

7. Lastly, cook the porcini in butter. In a stick-proof pan, place 2 3/4 tablespoons of butter and the rosemary. Add the finely sliced porcini, stir and sauté until golden brown.

If you like porcini, you can cook them directly with the snails. Chiodini di Pioppo mushrooms, which grow abundantly on our plain, are also very good. In the recipe given here, the unmistakeable flavour of mushrooms combines beautifully with the intense tang of snails.

In the glass: suggested wines

This dish goes very well with a structured white wine: Batàr – Querciabella (Tuscany); Terre di Franciacorta Chardonnay – Ca' del Bosco (Lombardy); Chardonnay Lowengang – Lageder (Alto Adige); Riesling Clos Sainte-Hune – Trimbach (Alsace, France).

dal Pescatore

Foie gras with summer fruit

Ingredients

Foie gras, either goose or duck,
4 slices 1/2″ thick
Rosemary
Sage
Marsala rock salt
Butter 2 teaspoons

FOR THE SAUCE
Butter 2 tablespoons
Passito dessert wine 4 tablespoons
Beef stock 4 tablespoons
Rosemary 1 twig
Black cherries
Raspberries
Traditional balsamic vinegar
from Modena a few drops

Fruit

Time: **8'**

Preparation

1. For the sauce, melt 2 tablespoons of butter in an aluminium pan, add the passito wine and bring to the boil until the liquid has evaporated and the sugar, sticking to the sides of the pan, has caramelised.
When a thin layer of toasted sugar has formed, wet the sides of the pan with the stock to detach the sugar, and aromatise the mixture with the rosemary. Simmer and stir until the sauce is soft and velvety. Add the traditional balsamic vinegar from Modena, the black cherries and the raspberries, then set aside.

2. In a teflon pan, melt 2 teaspoons of butter, let it brown and when it begins to sizzle add the foie gras. Then lower the heat, to cook it slowly but perfectly.

3. Using a steel spatula, turn the slices of foie gras, salt and flavour them with the sage and rosemary, making sure that both sides are crunchy and golden and the inside is hot.

4. Serve with the previously prepared sauce, finishing with a few grains of Marsala salt and with fruit as desired.

Foie gras is the real test of a cook; excellent results can be attained only through great experience. So don't be discouraged, keep trying!

In the glass: suggested wines

To accompany this dish you can serve the passito wine used for the sauce or, in alternative, one of the following: Muffato della Sala – Castello della Sala (Umbria); Le Pergole del Sole – Cavalchina (Veneto); Vin Santo Occhio di Pernice – Avignonesi (Tuscany). Other good choices are: SGN Pinot Gris Altenbourg Dom Weinbach – C. Faller et Filles (Alsace, France); SGN Gewürztraminer – Trimbach (Alsace, France); Château d'Yquem – Sauternes (Bordeaux, France).

dal Pescatore

Parmesan tuiles

Ingredients

Grated Parmesan
 or Grana Padano cheese 1/4 cup
Butter to grease the pan

Time: 0,3'

Preparation

1. Grease a pan lightly with butter and put it over the fire. When the butter is sizzling hot, swirl the pan to eliminate any excess liquid.

2. Add the grated Parmesan to the pan in well-spaced heaps; level them to the same thickness to form small wafers. Cook over moderate heat until the bottom of each wafer is straw-yellow.

3. Using a wooden stick and with the aid of tongs or a sharp knife, lift each wafer and rest it on the stick to shape the tuile.

4. Serve at once as appetisers with an aperitif.

The two key elements for the success of this recipe are, as always, mastery of the technique and high quality of the ingredients. Don't worry if the results are disappointing the first time. With a little practice and using top-quality cheese, you will soon be able to make this delicious appetiser.

In the glass: suggested wines

Serve the tuiles with whatever aperitif you prefer: a Franciacorta Brut, a Trento Doc or Prosecco; but also a Cartizze or a great Champagne.

Egg and nettles frittata

Ingredients (serves 6)

Nettles 1/2 lb
Eggs 4
Onion 1
Grated Parmesan 2/3 cup
Butter 3 1/3 tablespoons
Salt
Pepper

Mixed vegetables pickled in oil
Mixed vegetables pickled in vinegar

Time: **10'**

Preparation

1. In a non-stick pan, sauté the sliced onion in the butter, then add the nettles, after having washed and blanched them.

2. Beat the eggs, add the grated Parmesan, salt and pepper. Pour the mixture into a pan heated over a high flame.

3. With a wooden spatula, stir the mixture until it begins to thicken; then turn it from the outside towards the centre, to keep it soft but firm enough to turn.

4. Turn the frittata: to impress your friends, practice flipping it in the air, otherwise you can turn it with the help of a lid.

5. Cook the frittata until lightly and evenly browned.

6. Serve on a hot dish, accompanied by mixed vegetables pickled in oil or vinegar.

Since a frittata can be made quickly and easily, it is the ideal dish to serve in case of unexpected guests. If you are careful to carry out each each step of the recipe correctly, you will obtain excellent results. And don't forget: the secret of a good frittata is cooking it over high heat. A local proverb, in fact, says, "Pèss e fritada fòec al la disperada" (Fish and frittata, desperately hot).

In the glass: suggested wines

This dish is ideally accompanied by a white wine.
The choice is ample, ranging from Veneto wines, fresh, light and with a fruity scent, to the whites of Lombardy, which fully express the nature of the Colli Morenici, or again, from the classic wines of Collio to those of Franciacorta. Here are our suggestions: Capitel Foscarino – R. Anselmi (Veneto); Pinot Grigio del Friuli – Grandi Gabbana (Friuli Venezia Giulia); Garda Garganega Paroni – La Prendina (Lombardy); Franciacorta Satèn – Barone Pizzini (Lombardy); Chateau Greysac Bordeaux Blanc (Bordeaux, France).

Vegetable pastry with asparagus and peas

Ingredients

Pastry dough 2/3 cup
Small onion 1
Celery 1 stalk
Peas 1/2 cup
Asparagus 3/4 lb
Carrots 1/5 lb
Butter 1/4 cup
Breadcrumbs 2 teaspoons
Stock 1 ladle
Basil, a few leaves
Egg yolk 1
Rock salt

Seasonal vegetables

Time: 30'
plus pastry prep time

Preparation

1. Put the pastry dough on a linen or cotton cloth lightly dusted with flour and roll it with a rolling pin to a thickness of 1/8".

2. In a saucepan, melt 2 tablespoons of butter, add a tablespoon of breadcrumbs and spread the mixture over the dough.

3. With the rest of the butter, lightly brown the finely sliced onion and celery. Add the previously cleaned asparagus, the diced carrots, and the stock. Cook over moderate heat for a few minutes, until the asparagus is done but still crunchy.

4. Add the peas and a few leaves of basil, continue cooking for 2-3 minutes, then remove from the fire and let cool to luke-warm.

5. Spread this mixture on the round of dough; with the aid of the linen cloth, fold it over and close it.

6. Gloss the surface with beaten egg yolk and grains of rock salt.

7. Bake in an oven preheated to 340 °F/170 °C until golden brown.

8. Slice the filled pastry and place the slices on a plate, garnishing it with seasonal vegetables.

In preparing this dish, make sure that the different flavours are perfectly balanced. As in many recipes, in fact, this is a crucial ingredient for successful results.

In the glass: suggested wines

Bianco Cervaro della Sala (Umbria); Chardonnay – Produttori di Colterenzio (Alto Adige); Vermentino – Capichera (Sardinia); Capitel Croce – R. Anselmi (Veneto); Soave la Rocca – Pieropan (Veneto); Franciacorta Satèn – Ferghettina (Lombardy); Pouilly Fumé Silex – D. Daguenau (Loire, France); Brut Vieille France – A. Le Brun (Champagne, France); Muscat Goldert – Dom. Zind Humbrecht (Alsace, France); Meursault Charmes – Comtes Lafon (Bourgogne, France).

dal Pescatore
Santini

Red radicchio tart with Bagna Cauda

Ingredients (serves 6)

Pastry dough 1/2 lb
Red radicchio of Verona or Treviso 1 lb
Garlic 1 clove
Extra-virgin olive oil from Romagna 3 tablespoons
Breadcrumbs 2 tablespoons
Egg yolk 1
Salt
Pepper

FOR THE BAGNA CAUDA
Butter 2 2/3 tablespoons
Extra-virgin olive oil 2 1/2 tablespoons
Small anchovies (packed in salt) 2
Garlic 2 cloves
Milk 8 tablespoons

Time: **20'**
plus cooling time

Preparation

1. Roll the pastry dough to a thickness of 1/8". Butter a pie pan and line it with a round of dough cut to size; set aside in the refrigerator.

2. In the meantime, heat the olive oil in a wide pan, add the garlic cut in half and stir to flavour the olive oil. Add the washed and dried radicchio leaves; salt and pepper. Simmer over low heat for a few minutes, until the vegetables have wilted.

3. Sprinkle the dough in the pie pan with breadcrumbs and place the radicchio on it: the dough will absorb the dampness of the vegetables, ensuring that it cooks well.

4. Seal the tart with another round of dough, prepared previously, and brush the surface with beaten egg yolk.

5. Bake at 345 °F/175 °C until the surface of the pie is crunchy and golden.

6. For the bagna cauda, melt the butter in a terracotta pot. Add the milk, half a clove of garlic, the olive oil and lastly the anchovies, deboned, well cleaned and chopped fine. Sauté these ingredients for a few minutes.

7. Remove the tart from the oven, let it cool and then slice it. Serve accompanied by the bagna cauda.

Savoury pies, widely represented in the traditional cooking of Southern Italy, are not found in the cuisine of Lombardy, and of Mantua in particular, where the frittata is king. Our proposal is thus a recipe that combines the idea of a dish from "elsewhere" with the ingredients typical of our territory.

In the glass: suggested wines

You can balance the intense and slightly bitter tang of the radicchio with a wine that is structured but not too austere, or with an aromatic Alsatian. Our proposals are: Vintage Tunina – Jermann (Friuli Venezia Giulia); Amedeo Custoza Superiore – Cavalchina (Veneto); Lugana Riserva – Zenato (Veneto); Riesling Cuvée F. Emile – Trimbach (Alsace, France).

Baby squid salad with tomatoes and basil

Ingredients

Baby squid 2/3 lb
Camone or Marinda tomatoes 4
Celery, fennel, basil
Lemon juice
Extra-virgin olive oil from Lake Garda 3 tablespoons
Salt
Pepper

Time: 10'
plus cleaning of the squids

Preparation

1. Clean the squid thoroughly; chop the tomatoes in cubes 1/3" per side and place them in a bowl-shaped serving dish with handles.

2. In a pot, boil abundant water with celery and fennel to aromatise it. Place the squid in a strainer; plunge them into the boiling water for 30 seconds and then rinse with cold water.

3. Mix the squid with the tomatoes and dress the salad with extra-virgin olive oil, salt, pepper and lemon juice. Lastly, add the basil leaves. Let the flavours blend for a few minutes and then serve.

This is a very delicate dish, with the flavours and fragrance of springtime brought by the Camone or Marinda tomatoes, filled with the sun of our islands; the former are in fact grown in Sicily, the latter in Sardinia.

In the glass: suggested wines

To heighten the flavour of this recipe, choose an elegant, fruity white wine. We suggest: Petite Arvine – Les Crêtes (Valle d'Aosta); Sauvignon – B. Brandolini d'Adda (Friuli Venezia Giulia); Cometa Fiano – Planeta (Sicily); Puligny Montrachet – J.M. Boillot (Bourgogne, France); Champagne Brut – B. Paillard (Champagne, France).

dal Pescatore
Santini

Tomato, aubergine, basil and extra-virgin olive oil compote

Ingredients (serves 4-6)

Ripe, full-flavoured tomatoes 8
Long aubergine 1
Extra-virgin olive oil 3 tablespoons
Fresh basil (with its flowers)
Salt

FOR THE GELATINE
Vegetable gelatine 1 teaspoon
Vegetable stock 1 ladle
Ice 1/4 cup

Time: 20'
plus cooling time

Preparation

1. Peel the aubergine and slice it finely with a food slicer to obtain as many slices as necessary to line a small ceramic terrine.

2. Peel the tomatoes cold using a sharp knife; squeeze them with the hands to press out the seeds and the excess liquid.

3. Using an aluminium frying pan for faster cooking and crunchier aubergines, pour into it a few drops of olive oil; when the oil is very hot, add the aubergine slices and sauté until golden brown.

4. Line the terrine with the aubergine slices, fill it with the crushed tomatoes and seal it by folding over the ends of the slices.

5. Place on it 2-3 basil leaves, reserving the flowers to garnish the dish just before serving.

6. For the gelatine, bring the stock to the boil, melt the gelatine in it and remove from the heat; then add the ice to lower the temperature and shorten the preparation time.

7. Using a knife, spread the gelatine over the tomato and aubergine mixture, filling all of the spaces. Press well to expel the air.

8. Refrigerate for at least an hour. Then turn out onto a platter and serve with extra-virgin olive oil. Lastly, garnish the dish with the basil flowers.

The best tomatoes, basil in flower and Tuscan extra-virgin olive oil – all primary flavours for this exquisitely summery dish, delicious but not particularly easy to make.

In the glass: suggested wines

Franciacorta Brut – Ca' del Bosco (Lombardy); Franciacorta Comarì del Salem – Uberti (Lombardy); Trento Classico Riserva Giulio Ferrari (Trentino); Brut Riserva Elena – Podere Rocche dei Manzoni (Piemonte); Champagne Brut – B. Paillard (Champagne, France); Champagne Substance – J. Selosse (Champagne, France).

Anchovy tart

Ingredients

Extra-fresh anchovies 2/3 lb
Lightly salted or sweet pastry dough 1/4 lb
Butter
Tomato 1
Breadcrumbs 2 tablespoons
Garlic 1 clove
Finely chopped parsley 1 tablespoon
Salted anchovy 1

Mixed salad
Oil
Fresh onions
Traditional balsamic vinegar from Modena (or Reggio Emilia) a few drops

Time: 50'

Preparation

1. Butter a 7" round mould and line it with the disk of pastry dough.

2. Sauté in the butter a clove of unpeeled garlic; add the salted anchovy, thoroughly cleaned and deboned; stir until dissolved, add the breadcrumbs and parsley.

3. Pour this mixture into the mould and cover it with a layer of dough.

4. Clean the fresh anchovies well, removing the heads and the central bone.

5. Place the anchovies in the mould, along with some slices of fresh tomato and the breadcrumbs flavoured with garlic and parsley. Proceed in this way, forming layers and utilising all of the anchovies.

6. Place in a preheated oven (350 °F/180 °C) and bake for about 15 minutes. When the tart begins to brown, remove it from the oven.

7. Serve with a salad of mixed greens and fresh onions, olive oil and traditional balsamic vinegar from Modena or Reggio Emilia.

This rustic tart can also be made with freshwater fish (Rutilus aula) in place of anchovies.

In the glass: suggested wines

Since this dish calls for a wine that has a strong taste but is also elegant, we suggest accompanying it with a Champagne or a Franciacorta. Our proposals are: Brut Rosé Dom Ruinart – Ruinart (Champagne, France); Brut Vieille France – A. Le Brun (Champagne, France); Brut Grande Année – Bollinger (Champagne, France); Franciacorta Brut Collezione – Cavalleri (Lombardy); Franciacorta Brut Riserva – Ca' del Bosco (Lombardy).

dal Pescatore

Fried pioppini mushrooms

Ingredients

Pioppini mushrooms 1/2 lb
Flour 3/4 cup
Extra-virgin olive oil for frying 4 cups
Rock salt

Radicchietto
Young green leaf salad
White wine vinegar a few drops

Time: 20'

Preparation

1. Clean and wash the mushrooms, then simmer them for a few minutes in a large pot of boiling water.

2. Drain them and place them on kitchen paper to dry.

3. Lightly dust the mushrooms with flour and fry them in hot oil.

4. Sprinkle with rock salt and serve piping hot.

5. You can accompany the fried mushrooms with finely sliced radicchietto or young green leaf salad, dressed with white wine vinegar.

For this recipe, many different varieties of mushroom can be used (make sure they are all edible!). I remember that around Trento, during the harvest season, the farmers used to sell small amounts of everything they had found as "mixed mushrooms".

In the glass: suggested wines

Franciacorta Brut Cabochon – Monte Rossa (Lombardy); Franciacorta Riserva Vittorio Moretti – Bellavista (Lombardy); Franciacorta Comarì del Salem – Uberti (Lombardy); Gaja e Rey Chardonnay – Gaja (Piemonte); Puligny-Montrachet – E. Sauzet (Bourgogne, France); Ridge Chardonnay Santa Cruz Mountains – Santa Cruz Mountain (California).

Potato tuiles

Ingredients

Water 2 ladles
Flour 1 cup
Sieved potatoes 1/2 cup
Extra-virgin olive oil 4 scant tablespoons
Finely chopped fresh onions 1 tablespoons
Finely chopped fresh rosemary 1 twig
Salt 1/4 teaspoon

Time: 40'

Preparation

1. Fill a small pan with cold water and cook a large potato in it. When the potato is done, pass it through a sieve.

2. Pour the water into a terrine; add the flour, the sieved potato, 2 tablespoons of extra-virgin olive oil and the salt.

3. Lightly brown the chopped onions and half of the rosemary in 1 tablespoon of olive oil; add to the flour and potato mixture and work well with a spoon to form a rather sticky dough.

4. With the aid of a spoon, drop small heaps of the potato dough onto sheets of oven paper, lightly flatten each heap and sprinkle with a few drops of olive oil (2 teaspoons). Bake in an oven preheated to 350 °F/180 °C for 15 minutes.

5. Remove from the oven and serve.

This dish makes an excellent appetiser, suitable even for those affected by yeast intolerance.

Cornmeal wafers

Ingredients

Whole-grain cornmeal 1 2/3 cups
Water 3 ladles
Extra-virgin olive oil 2 tablespoons
Salt

Time: 45'

Preparation

1. In a non-stick pot, mix the water, the olive oil and a little salt and bring to the boil. Sprinkle in the cornmeal a little at a time, stirring constantly with a wire whisk; cook for 8-10 minutes.

2. Cover large flat platters with oven paper. Using a spoon, pour the cornmeal mixture onto the oven paper and cover it entirely with another sheet of paper. Roll the mixture with a rolling pin to form a very thin layer of dough.

3. Remove the piece of oven paper on the top and bake the dough for at least 15-20 minutes at 350 °F/180 °C. When half-cooked, pull out of the oven and cut the dough with a long knife so that, when it is done, it will separate into regularly shaped wafers.

This dish, suitable for everyone, is an excellent substitute for bread for those affected by gluten intolerance.

First courses

WITH FIRST COURSES AND EVEN MORE IN PASTA-MAKING, the best results cannot be achieved merely by a numerical calculation of amounts. The variables involved are so finely balanced that increasing the amount of one ingredient often means having to decrease that of another. Seasonal variations too (as in egg yolks, for example,

which are more watery in summer than in winter) have an influence on the result; these factors cannot be corrected merely by using scales. The cook must trust his or her own sensitivity, educated through experience, and even by making mistakes. In the following recipes, the proportions depend on the quality of the products we use and on our "sensitivity". Do you prefer pasta that is more elastic and pale yellow in colour? Increase the amount of egg whites and decrease the amount of yolks. Or do you like pasta that is fragrant, less elastic and a brighter yellow? Then use more egg yolks. The absolutely perfect recipe does not exist. There exists a proportion that can make us happy, satisfying both our palates and our senses.

Ravioli with guineafowl and porcini mushrooms

Ingredients

FOR THE FILLING
Breast of guineafowl 1
Celery 1 stalk
Fresh onion 1/2 small
Butter 1/4 cup
Water 1 ladle
Stock 1 ladle
Grand Marnier
Salt and pepper

FOR THE PORCINI
Porcini mushrooms
5 medium-sized
Chopped celery 1 tablespoon
Chopped fresh onion
1/2 tablespoon
Finely chopped parsley
1 tablespoon
Extra-virgin olive oil

FOR THE PASTA
Egg yolks 3
Flour 2/3 cup

Time: 40'
plus filling resting time
and making of the pastry

Preparation

1. Cut the breast of guineafowl into small cubes; brown them in a pan with the butter, the chopped fresh onion and celery for 30 seconds over high heat. Add the Grand Marnier and, if you like, half a cup of red wine, then add the stock, water, salt and pepper, and simmer for about 10 minutes.

2. Remove from the heat and blend these ingredients in the blender, adding a little stock if necessary to form a soft mixture.
Let the filling cool and then refrigerate it for about an hour, so that it assumes a firm consistency.

3. For the pasta, add the egg yolks to the flour and knead together very well, then refrigerate the dough for 30 minutes. Roll it extremely thin (less than 1/16" thick) and cut it into squares 2" per side using a smooth pastry cutter.

4. At the centre of each square of dough, place a teaspoon of filling and close it to form the ravioli.

5. Cut 4 porcini into small regular cubes; sauté them in a pan with the extra-virgin olive oil, chopped celery and fresh onion. Flavour with salt and pepper and add a tablespoon of chopped parsley when half-done.

6. Cook the ravioli in boiling salted water for 3 minutes. Drain and lightly toss them in a pan with extra-virgin olive oil, a clove of garlic for its fragrance only, and the last porcino, cut into 8 wedges.

7. Place the cubed porcini at the centre of a platter to form a circle, put the ravioli on them and decorate with the porcini wedges.

In the glass: suggested wines

Bianco – Massa Vecchia (Tuscany); Trebbiano d'Abruzzo – Valentini (Abruzzo); Riesling "Clos Sainte Hune" –Trimbach (Alsace, France); Puligny-Montrachet Le Clovoillon – Dom. Lefleive (France); Vitovska – Vodopivec (Friuli).

Egg pasta tortelli with ricotta and sweet herbs

Ingredients

FOR THE FILLING
Ricotta 1/2 lb
Grated Parmesan 2 tablespoons
Herbs 25 leaves
Nutmeg
Salt and pepper

FOR THE PASTA
Egg yolks 3
Flour 3/4 cup

FOR THE DRESSING
Butter 1/4 cup
Grated Parmesan

Time: **20'**
plus making of the pasta

Preparation

1. Blend the herbs in a blender with a very little cold water.

2. Strain them and use the solid part remaining in the strainer to prepare the filling of the tortelli, adding to it the strained ricotta, the Parmesan, salt, pepper and nutmeg. Mix well.

3. Knead together the egg yolks and the flour; refrigerate the dough for 30 minutes. Roll the dough very fine and cut it into rectangles 4" x 2".

4. Heap a little of the filling at the centre of each rectangle. fold the dough and, using a pasta cutter or a mould, shape it into tortelli.

5. Cook the tortelli for 3 minutes in boiling salty water and serve them dressed with melted butter and grated Parmesan.

In the glass: suggested wines

Pinot Grigio bio – Brandolini d'Adda (Friuli); Pinot Bianco Alto-Adige – Giorgio Grai (Friuli); Madre Perla – Perla del Garda (Lombardy); Puligny-Montrachet Les Enseignères J.F. Coche Dury (France).

Catalan-style lobster with creamed cannellini beans, mangos and mixed green salad

Ingredients

Lobster 2 1/2 lbs
Green beans 5
Snow peas 2
Mango 1 slice 1/5" thick
Celery 1/2 stalk
Juice of 1/2 lemon
Extra-virgin olive oil
Salt and pepper

FOR THE CHERRY TOMATO CONFITS
Date tomatoes 10
Oregano
Salt and sugar

FOR THE SAUCE
Dried cannellini beans 1 1/4 cups
Celery 1/2 stalk
Fresh onion 1 tablespoon
Bay leaf 1
Vegetable stock
Extra-virgin olive oil

Time: 2h15'
plus soaking of the beans

Preparation

1. Plunge the lobster into boiling water and cook for 5 minutes, then remove the flesh from the shell.

2. Cut the flesh into cubes 3/4" per side ; marinate them in a vinaigrette made of extra-virgin olive oil, lemon juice, pepper and salt.

3. Meanwhile, cut the mango into small cubes 1/5" per side, chop the celery fine and cut the green beans and snow peas into pieces (after having boiled and cooled them in iced water).

4. To prepare the confit, slice the tomatoes lengthwise into quarters, place them in a pan lined with oven paper and sprinkle with extra-virgin olive oil, a pinch of oregano, one of salt and one of sugar. Bake them at 195 °F/90 °C for 1 hour.

5. When the tomatoes are done, add them to the lobster along with the vegetables and mix delicately.

6. For the sauce, soak the cannellini beans overnight, then drain and sauté them in a pot with extra-virgin olive oil, the chopped celery, fresh onion and bay leaf. After 1 minute, add water and stock and simmer until the beans are very soft. Taste for salt and blend these ingredients. Strain them to form a soft, smooth cream without lumps; correct the density by adding a little water if necessary.

7. Serve in a soup tureen, placing the Catalan-style lobster in the centre, surrounded by the creamed beans.
This dish can be garnished, in season, with beet chips and crunchy artichokes.

In the glass: suggested wines

Franciacorta Satèn – Ca' del Bosco (Lombardy); Brut – Costaripa (Lombardy); Blanc de Millenaire – Charles Heidsieck (Champagne, France); Vintage Millesimé Rosé – Dom Perignon (Champagne, France).

Egg pasta tagliatelle with mint and chili pepper

Ingredients

FOR THE PASTA
Flour 00 2/3 cup
Egg yolks 3

FOR THE SAUCE
Extra-virgin olive oil from Lake Garda 4 tablespoons
Spring onion 1
Chili pepper 1
Celery 1 stalk
Mint leaves 10
Stock 1 ladle
Water 1 ladle
Salt

Time: 35'

Preparation

1. For the pasta, mix the egg yolks with the flour and work well. With a rolling pin, roll out 2 pieces of dough 16" long, with thickness of 1/3" and 1/2" - 3/4" thick. Cut the dough lengthwise into ribbons 1/8" wide.

2. For the sauce, pour abundant extra-virgin olive oil into an aluminium pan and add the sliced spring onion, chili pepper, and celery; sauté for a few minutes, then add the mint leaves, stock and water. Simmer for 5 minutes. Blend, strain and set aside (you will use this sauce in cooking the tagliatelle).

3. Plunge the tagliatelle into boiling salted water for one minute, drain them, then finish cooking (about 4-5 minutes) in the sauce prepared previously. As the pasta cooks you can add more mint leaves broken into bits.

4. Serve the tagliatelle in a small round mould; decorate with the sauce they have cooked in.

This is a traditional dish from the Po Valley: here, tagliatelle are also served in broth.

In the glass: suggested wines

The ideal accompaniment for this dish is a Moscato from Alto Adige, dry and fragrant, or if you prefer, a fresh, light sparkling white wine.
We suggest: Müller Thurgau – Cantina di Novacella (Alto Adige).
In alternative: Gewürztraminer Reserve – A. Kientzler (Alsace, France); Prosecco di Valdobbiadene – Aneri (Veneto); Prosecco di Valdobbiadene – Bisol (Veneto); Prosecco di Valdobbiadene – N. Franco (Veneto).

dal Pescatore
Santini

Pumpkin tortelli

Ingredients

Pumpkin 1 1/3 cups
Salt
Sugar
Butter 1/4 cup

FOR THE FILLING
Pumpkin cooked and sieved 2/3 cup
Chopped amaretti 20
Mustard fruits 3 1/3 tablespoons
Grated Parmesan 1 heaping tablespoon
Salt
Pepper
Nutmeg, cloves, cinnamon

FOR THE PASTA
Flour 00 1 cup
Egg yolks 4

Butter
Grated Parmesan

Time: 2h

Preparation

1. Choose a pumpkin, cut a thick slice of it and cook it in lightly salted water for 30 minutes, or until soft as a boiled potato. Add a little sugar to make up for what has been lost in the cooking. Remove the slice of pumpkin from the water, peel it and pass it through a food mill.

2. For the filling, add to the mashed pumpkin the amaretti, the chopped mustard fruit, grated Parmesan and all of the spices. Set aside to rest in a cool place until time to start making the pasta.

3. For the pasta, heap the flour on a breadboard, leaving a well in the centre; place the egg yolks in the well and work these ingredients to form a smooth, porous dough.

4. Roll the dough thin with a pasta machine or rolling pin; cut it into squares 3" per side. Heap a little of the filling (about 1/3 to 1/2 tablespoon) onto each square and close diagonally, bringing the two ends together, then fold again and press the edges firmly down around the filling.

5. Cook the tortelli in boiling water for 5 minutes; dress with butter and grated Parmesan and serve.

Pumpkin tortelli, a classic in the cuisine of the plains, are found from Ferrara to Cremona, and are the subject of culinary challenges destined to leave every cook certain of having made the world's best tortelli! Today we use less butter and fewer amaretti than in the traditional version. The final result, however, depends above all on the pumpkin. Grandmother Bruna insists that you must choose a very heavy one. The variety utilised is yellow, slightly flattened and has evident ribbing.

In the glass: suggested wines

Wines to go with this dish are suggested by my friend the sommelier Roberto Ferrari from the legendary Bersagliere di Goito. With him and Tano Martini from the Cigno restaurant in Mantua, we have visited, in Italy and abroad, hundreds of wineries and sampled many wines over the last thirty years.
I thought it would be interesting, then, to hear his opinion on two classic recipes. For the pumpkin tortelli, Roberto recommends: Passito Bianco, I Capitelli – R. Anselmi (Veneto); Nussbaumer Gewürztraminer – Produttori di Termeno (Alto Adige); Riesling Spatlese Rothenpfad – C. Busch (Mosella, Germany); Gewürztraminer Altenbour Cuvée – Laurence Dom. Weinbach (Alsace, France).

Sweet onion soup with slices of citrus-flavoured foie gras

Ingredients

White onions 2
Butter 1 1/2 tablespoons
Stock 2 ladles
Water 2 ladles
Foie gras 3 1/2 oz
Rosemary 1 twig
Lemon rind 1/4
Salt
Pepper

Time: **20'**

Preparation

1. In an aluminium pot, melt the butter, brown the finely chopped onions in it, then add the water and stock. Salt and pepper.

2. Boil over high heat for 10 minutes, then blend and strain to form a perfectly smooth, even soup.

3. In a stick-proof pan, sauté the foie gras sliced in small pieces; flavour it with minced rosemary and lemon rind.

4. Add the foie gras to the soup and serve.

Foie gras is the main ingredient of this recipe. The sweetish taste of the onions and the citrus flavoured of the lemon rind heighten and enhance its taste. This is an excellent winter-time dish, to be served from autumn to spring.

In the glass: suggested wines

To accompany this recipe we suggest an aromatic white wine, or in any case a wine of harmonious taste such as a Müller Thurgau Valle d'Isarco (Alto Adige) or a Gewürztraminer, also from Alto Adige. Alternatively, you can choose an extra dry Champagne.

Pigeon ravioli scented with thyme and Norcia black truffles

Ingredients

FOR THE FILLING
Pigeon (about 1 lb) 1
Celery 1 small stalk
Small spring onion 1
Butter 1/4 cup
Water 1 ladle
Stock 1 ladle
Brandy
Salt
Pepper

FOR THE PASTA
Egg yolks 3
Flour 3/4 cup

Melted butter
Thyme
Black truffles 1 oz

Time: **20'**
plus making of the pasta

Preparation

1. For the filling, debone the pigeon and remove the skin. Sauté the meat in a pan with the butter, brandy, spring onion and celery over high heat for 30 seconds. Add the stock and water and simmer for 10-15 minutes; add salt and pepper. Remove the meat from the pan juices.
Blend the pigeon meat with the vegetables and 2 tablespoons of the pan juices, to make the filling for the ravioli.

2. For the pasta, mix together the eggs and flour and work them well to form a dough. Roll out the dough with a rolling pin to form a rectangle 1/16" thick. Using a pastry cutter, cut the dough into squares about 2" per side. Heap some of the filling at the centre of each square and close it in the preferred shape (to form ravioli, tortellini, or crescents).

3. Cook the ravioli in salted boiling water until they rise to the surface, soft and fluffy.

4. Serve them with melted butter, thyme and black truffles, finishing with the remaining sauce.

Ravioli are a leitmotif of Italian cooking, especially in the north. The filling can be made with a wide variety of ingredients, ranging from meat to vegetables. The recipe given here is based on the full-flavoured taste of pigeon meat and the unique, unmistakeable flavour of Norcia truffles.

In the glass: suggested wines

A structured white, a spumante with character or a mellow red wine all go very well with this dish. We suggest: Franciacorta Riserva Vittorio Moretti (Lombardy); Trento Classico Riserva Giulio Ferrari (Trentino); Tignanello aged at least 6 years (Tuscany); Pinot Nero – F. Hass (Alto Adige).

Tortelli filled with fior di ricotta, pecorino cheese and melted Parmesan

Ingredients

FOR THE FILLING
Robiola cheese 1/4 cup
Aged Tuscan Pecorino cheese 3/4 cup
Parmesan 1/2 cup
Sheep's milk ricotta 1/2 cup

FOR THE PASTA
Egg yolks 6
Flour 00 1 1/4 cups

Butter 1/4 cup
Parmesan 1/2 cup

Time: **20'**
plus filling cooling time

Preparation

1. For the filling, grate the pecorino cheese and the Parmesan and pass the Ricotta and the robiola cheese through a strainer. Mix these ingredients in a deep, rounded bowl and set aside to rest in a cool place for about 30 minutes.

2. For the pasta, work the egg yolks and flour together to form a smooth, even dough, then roll it out with a rolling pin. Place small heaps of the filling on the dough, evenly spaced. Cover with another layer of dough. With a pasta cutter, cut out round, square or crescent-shaped tortelli, as preferred.

3. Plunge the tortelli gently into a pot of boiling salted water. When they rise to the surface, fluffy and light, they are done.

4. Melt the butter and pour it while still very hot onto a large serving dish; sprinkle with Parmesan.

5. Arrange the tortelli on the dish, one beside another, grate over them more Parmesan and finish by dribbling a little more butter over them, so that the Parmesan will melt on the pasta and the dish will be much more fragrant.

In autumn you can complete this recipe with a grating of white Alba truffles. The precious tubers will be greatly enhanced by the simplicity of this first course. In springtime instead, you can garnish it with grated black truffles.

In the glass: suggested wines

With this first course we suggest: Dolcetto di Dogliani Briccolero – Chionetti (Piemonte); Chiaretto del Garda – Costaripa (Lombardy); Cerasuolo d'Abruzzo – Valentini (Abruzzo). It also goes beautifully with a classic Meursault Les Rougeots – J.F. Coche-Dury (Bourgogne, France).

Agnoli in chicken soup (Grandma Bruna's recipe)

Ingredients (serves 4-6)

Beef (shoulder) 1 lb
Hen 1/2
Aromatic herbs 1 bunch
Salt

FOR THE FILLING
Onion 1
Butter 1/4 cup
Rosemary 1 twig
Sage a few leaves
Salt
Pepper

FOR THE PASTA
Egg yolks 6
Flour 00 1 1/4 cups

Time: $2^h10'$
plus agnoli cooking time

Preparation

1. Put the meat in a large pot, with a bunch of parsley, celery and a small carrot. Cover with abundant cold salted water. Simmer over low heat for about 2 hours.

2. For the filling, while the broth is cooking, sauté the sliced onion in the butter, add a twig of rosemary and a few leaves of sage; brown gently for 5 minutes. Remove the onion and aromatic herbs from the pan and add to it the boiled beef with a little of its stock. Continue cooking for 15 minutes. Add salt and pepper to taste and pass through a meat grinder at least twice.

3. For the pasta, mix the eggs and flour and work them together to form a smooth dough. With the rolling pin, roll the dough out fine. Using a pasta cutter, cut it into squares 2" per side, heap some of the filling onto each square and close it in the shape of a ring.

4. Cook the agnoli in the broth; serve in a soup tureen placed at the centre of the table.

In the Po Valley this is a dish for festive occasions, the test of a cook's excellence and ability to attain a perfect balance of flavours (a little secret for doing so consists of choosing the right cut of meat: the shoulder, veined in fat). I still remember my grandfather, who tasted first the broth, then the agnoli, and finally expressed his judgement. And often he added a dash of Lambrusco.

In the glass: suggested wines

With this dish you can serve a simple Lambrusco or a great wine, either young or aged, but preferably red. Each of the suggested wines has been tried with the agnoli and has combined with it in a unique, original manner, revealing its own unmistakeable character. And this confirms again the fact that the combining of food and wine is one of the most fascinating and variable aspects of dining at a restaurant. Here are our choices: Barolo Vigna Cappella di Santo Stefano – Rocche dei Manzoni (Piemonte); Barbaresco Camp Gros – Marchesi di Gresy (Piemonte); San Leonardo – C. Guerrieri Gonzaga (Trentino); Sassicaia – Marchese Incisa della Rocchetta (Tuscany); Sammarco – Castello dei Rampolla (Tuscany); Montevetrano – S. Imparato (Campania).

Fettucine with bass and baby squid

Ingredients

FOR THE PASTA
Egg yolks 6
Flour 00 1 1/4 cups
(if using ready-made pasta, 1/2 lb for 4 people)

FOR THE GREEN ONION SAUCE
Extra-virgin olive oil 4 tablespoons
Finely chopped spring onion 2 tablespoons
Lemon juice 1 teaspoon
Dry white wine
Stock 1 ladle
Water 1 ladle
Salt 1 pinch
Chopped celery 2 tablespoons

Bass 1/4 lb

FOR THE BABY SQUID
Baby squid 1/4 lb
Rosemary 1 twig
Thyme or mint 1 twig
Salt
Pepper

Time: 10'
plus drying of the pasta

Preparation

1. For the pasta, mix the egg yolks and flour and work well to form a smooth dough. Roll out 2 pieces of dough 15-16" long, with thickness of 1/3" and 1/2-3/4". Cut them longitudinally into ribbons 1/5" wide. Alternatively, cut it with a pasta making machine. Form 2 small heaps of fettucine and leave them to dry for about 2 hours on a wooden board.

2. For the spring onion sauce, pour the olive oil into an aluminium pan, add the chopped onion and sauté gently. Add the lemon juice, the white wine and a pinch of salt. Simmer for a few minutes, then add the stock and the water. Cook for about 2 minutes over moderate heat.

3. In the meantime, cook the pasta in a pot of boiling salted water for about one minute; drain it and add it to the pan with the spring onion sauce.

4. Cook and stir the pasta and sauce in the pan for about 4 minutes, making sure that the pasta is always well bathed in the liquid. The fettuccine will absorb the sauce, acquiring superb flavour. Finish the dish by adding the finely chopped green celery.

5. Add the finely sliced fillet of bass and continue cooking.

6. In a well-heated non-stick pan, sauté the baby squid with a little extra-virgin olive oil, the salt and a mixture of finely minced fresh rosemary and thyme. Stir and cook until the squid are crunchy.

7. Add the squid to the fettuccine and serve.

A light, summery dish to be made with the very freshest baby squid, just off the fishing boat.

In the glass: suggested wines

Chardonnay – Planeta (Sicily); Roero Arneis Renesio – Malvirà (Piemonte); Alto Adige Sauvignon Lafòa Schreckbichl – Produttori di Colterenzio (Alto Adige); Alto Adige Sauvignon Sanct Valentin – San Michele Appiano (Alto Adige); Collio Sauvignon Ronco delle mele – Venice (Friuli Venezia Giulia); Compte de Champagne – Taittinger (Champagne, France); Riesling Jahrgange – Weingut Forstmeister Geltz-Zilliken (Saarburg, Germany).

dal Pescatore

Risotto with catfish fillets, chives and skewers of crunchy eel

Ingredients

FOR THE CATFISH
Catfish 4 (or 8 fillets)
Butter 2 1/2 tablespoons
Finely chopped celery 4 tablespoons
Finely chopped spring onion 2 tablespoons
Nutmeg
Salt

FOR THE RISOTTO
Vialone Nano rice 1 cup
Butter 1/4 cup
Finely chopped fresh onion 1 teaspoon
Water 2 full ladles
Stock 2 full ladles
Chives
Grated Parmesan 1/2 cup
Salt
Pepper

Eel fillets 1/3 lb
Extra-virgin olive oil for frying

Time: 50'

Preparation

1. For the catfish, fillet the raw fish. In a non-stick pan, place the butter, chopped spring onion and chopped celery. Heat the saucepan and only when it is very hot, add the fish fillets, skin side down, and simmer over moderate heat for 10 minutes (5 minutes on one side and 5 minutes on the other). Grate the nutmeg ever the fillets and salt. Remove the skin from the fish and transfer the fillets to a dish.

2. For the risotto, stir the butter and chopped onion together in a pot and sauté for a few seconds. Then add the rice to the pot, stir and toast it for about 20 seconds. Then add a ladleful of stock and one of water, little at time, as the rice absorbs it. Cook for 3 minutes, add the catfish fillets and cook until done, for 10-12 minutes, adding the finely chopped chives at the end.

3. Stir and mix the Parmesan into the risotto, add a skewer of filleted eel fried in extra-virgin olive oil, and serve.

This risotto, with the flavours of the river, is dedicated to boatmen.

In the glass: suggested wines

For this plate a white wine is ideal. The skewered eel authorises the choice of a well-structured wine, without however excluding more sophisticated combinations. Our proposals are: Capitel Foscarino – R. Anselmi (Veneto); Colli Orientali del Friuli Terre Alte – L. Felluga (Friuli Venezia Giulia); Collio Pinot Bianco – Villa Russiz (Friuli Venezia Giulia); Alto Adige Sauvignon Sanct Valentin – San Michele Appiano (Alto Adige); Riesling Gran Cru – A. Kientzler (Alsace, France); Riesling Alsace – Hugel (Alsace, France).

VEGETABLE SOUP WITH GRAS PISTA'

Ingredients

Lentils 1/4 cup
Borlotti and Sorana beans 1/2 cup
Potatoes 1/2 cup
Onions 1/3 cup
Small carrot 1
Celery 1/2 stalk
Mixed greens (salad greens, spinach, etc.)
Sicilian extra-virgin olive oil 2 scant tablespoons
Butter 1/4 cup
Garlic 2 cloves
Salt
Pepper
Beef stock 4 cups
Water 1 ladle
Gras pista' 4 teaspoons

Time: 30'

Preparation

1. In a triple-bottom pan, put the olive oil and 1 1/2 tablespoons of butter. Melt the butter over moderate heat, then add 1 clove of garlic, the carrot, celery, onion and potato, all diced.

2. Sauté gently for a few minutes, then cover with the stock and the water. When the vegetables are done but still firm, add the beans and lentils and continue cooking for 20-25 minutes.

3. Lastly, add the other vegetables to the soup.

4. On a serving dish, serve the vegetables with their cooking broth and a small tablespoon of gras pista' (lard mashed with a knife and seasoned with finely chopped parsley and garlic, salt and pepper).

For this dish, choose only seasonal vegetables, of different colours if possible, to ensure good nutritional value and vitamins. Here is a little guide to choosing: white is the colour of vegetables that help to invigorate bone tissue and protect the lungs; orange vegetables instead have an antioxidant and provitaminic effect. Green vegetables are rich in chlorophyl, which facilitates the transmission of nerve impulses, and magnesium, a nutrient that helps to reduce high blood pressure. Purple vegetables contain a great amount of anthrocyanin, a substance that fluidizes the blood in the arteries and oxygenates the tissues. Red, instead, is the typical colour of vegetables having an antioxidant effect.

IN THE GLASS: SUGGESTED WINES

For this dish, a white wine is best: Gaja e Rey – Gaja (Piemonte); Gewürztraminer Lunare – Produttori di Termeno (Alto Adige); Vermentino – Capichera (Sardinia); Batàr – Querciabella (Tuscany); Meursault Perrières – J.F. Coche-Dury (Bourgogne, France).

Durum-wheat "occhi di lupo" with stracchino, tuna fish roe, basil and Pachino tomato sauce

Ingredients

"Occhi di lupo" or "mezze maniche" (short pasta) 48
Stracchino cheese (Angelo Croce) 2/3 cup
Extra-virgin olive oil 1 tablespoon
Grated Parmesan as desired
Salt and black pepper
Tuna fish roe
Basil a few leaves

FOR THE TOMATO SAUCE
Pachino tomatoes 1/2 lb
Finely chopped spring onion 1 tablespoon
Finely chopped celery 1 tablespoon
Extra-virgin olive oil 4 tablespoons
Vegetable stock 1 ladle

Time: 25'

Preparation

1. Cook the pasta in boiling salted water for about 9 minutes, drain it and dress it with extra-virgin olive oil, adding Parmesan as desired.

2. Place the stracchino, olive oil and pepper in a deep wide bowl and stuff the pasta with this filling.

3. Garnish the dish with thin slices of tuna-fish roe and small basil leaves (or chopped basil).

4. To prepare the sauce, put the oil, spring onion and celery in a sauce pan over high heat. Add the tomatoes cut in wedges and sauté for a few seconds; then add the stock and cook for 10 minutes. Blend and strain the sauce so that it is perfectly smooth and even.

5. Place the pasta in the dish and, if desired, complete with the tomato sauce at the centre.

This is a summer dish, to be served cold.

In the glass: suggested wines

Vintage Tunina – Jermann (Friuli Venezia Giulia); Colli di Luni Vermentino Boboli – Giacomelli (Liguria); Cervaro della Sala – Castello della Sala (Umbria); Puligny Montrachet Les Enseignéres – J.F. Coche-Dury (Bourgogne, France); Clos du Mesnil – Krug (Champagne, France).

Egg-pasta paccheri with ricotta, Trevigiano radicchio, baby squid and anchovy sauce

Ingredients

FOR THE PASTA
Egg yolks 3
Flour 00 3/4 cup

FOR THE FILLING AND GARNISH OF THE PACCHERI
Fresh cows' milk ricotta 2/3 cup
Late Trevigiano radicchio 2 heads
Baby squid 1/5 lb
Extra-virgin olive oil 4 tablespoons
Salt
Pepper
Sugar (optional)
Blended celery (optional)

FOR THE ANCHOVY SAUCE
Fresh milk 3/4 cup
Salted anchovies, washed and deboned 2
Celery 1 small stalk

Parmesan
Extra-virgin olive oil

Time: 1h05'
plus drying of the pasta

Preparation

1. For the pasta, add the egg yolks to the flour and work them together to form a smooth dough. Roll the dough to a thickness of 1/8"; cut it into rectangles about 2" by 4". Make the paccheri (considering 5 per portion), by folding together the shorter sides of the rectangles to form a sort of cylinder. Be sure to do this while the dough is still fresh enough to make the two edges to stick together. Let the pasta dry for about an hour.

2. For the filling, cut each head of radicchio into quarters; put them all into an aluminium pan with olive oil, salt an pepper. Simmer over moderate heat for 10-15 minutes, depending on the size of the radicchio head, until they are soft and fully wilted. Now blend the radicchio well and add the ricotta. Taste the filling; if it is too bitter, add a pinch of sugar or a small amount of blended celery.

3. For the anchovy sauce, simmer the milk with the anchovies and celery for 10 minutes over low heat, to reduce the sauce.

4. Cook the paccheri in boiling salted water; drain and dress lightly with extra-virgin olive oil and Parmesan. With the aid of tongs, stand the paccheri on end and stuff them with the hot filling.

5. Sauté the baby squid in a very hot pan, mix with the paccheri and serve.

This is a light first course with strong, sharp flavours.

In the glass: suggested wines

Gaja e Rey – Gaja (Piemonte); Cervaro della Sala – Castello della Sala (Umbria); Alto Adige Sauvignon Voglar Lugum – P. Dipoli (Alto Adige); Franciacorta Brut – Ca' del Bosco (Lombardy); Brut Vieille France – A. Le Brun (Champagne, Francia); Riesling Clos Sainte-Hune – Trimbach (Alsace, France); Coulée de Serrant – Joly (Bourgogne, Francia); Riesling Jahrgang Weiungut – Wittmann (Rheinhessen, Germany).

Risotto with saffron pistils and crunchy Puglia artichokes

Ingredients

Artichokes 2
Rosemary 1 twig
Butter 3 tablespoons
Salt

FOR THE RISOTTO
Vialone Nano rice 1 - 1 2/3 cups
Butter 1/4 cup
Small onion 1
Beef stock 6 cups
Saffron in pistils 1/2 teaspoon
Grated Parmesan 2 tablespoons

Time: **12'**

Preparation

1. Clean the artichokes by removing their outer leaves and cut them in half longitudinally. Remove the choke, if present, and slice them finely. Lightly brown the artichoke slices in an aluminium pan with butter and rosemary.

2. For the risotto, put half of the butter and the sliced onion in an aluminium saucepan; sauté gently over moderate heat and remove the onion. Add the rice all at once, stirring well with a wooden spoon to toast it lightly. Add a ladleful of boiling hot stock and, stirring constantly, cook the rice over high heat, adding more hot stock a little at a time as it dries.
A few minutes before it is perfectly done, add the saffron, which has been softened in a bowl with a little boiling hot stock. Stir until the rice becomes golden yellow.

3. When the risotto is done, add the remaining butter and the grated Parmesan; top with the crunchy artichokes.

There is a curious anecdote related to saffron. Signor Antoine Rucher, our friend and client, brought us one day a plant of Crocus sativus, *or saffron, and my father then began to produce it on a small scale, a production we are very proud of.*

In the glass: suggested wines

Our friend Tonino Trimboli, the great courtier, discoverer of outstanding French wines, suggests for this dish a white with a good degree of acidity (a Crémant d'Alsace of Vigneron will be excellent), or an Italian spumante. Or even a Champagne, composed of 70-80 percent Chardonnay grapes and the rest Pinot Nero, harmonises perfectly with the flavour of the artichokes and saffron.

Bean and pig's foot soup with onion-flavoured croutons

Ingredients (serves 6-8)

Medium-sized onions 2
Green celery 1 stalk
Carrot 1
Extra-virgin olive oil 10 tablespoons
Butter 1/4 cup
Garlic 1 clove
Potatoes 2
Pig's feet (or pork rind) 2
Borlotti beans, fresh or dried and soaked in water for 12 hrs 1/2 lb
Beef or vegetable stock 8 cups
Water 4 cups
Nutmeg
Cloves
Rosemary 1 twig
Tomato sauce 2 tablespoons
Croutons
Butter
Spring onion 1
Extra-virgin olive oil
Salt
Whole-grain black pepper

Time: $2^{h}30'$
plus soaking of the beans

Preparation

1. Break the onions, celery and carrots into pieces. In a large pan, put 1/2 cup of olive oil and the butter; heat on the stove.

2. Add the whole clove of garlic and the vegetables broken into pieces, sauté for a few minutes and add the whole potatoes, the two well-cleaned pig's feet and the soaked beans. Cover with the stock and water, add the tomato sauce, the spices, and lastly the rosemary. Cover and simmer over medium-low heat for 1 and 1/2 hours, until the vegetables are well done.

3. Remove a good part of the beans with some of the cooking liquid and blend them with an immersion blender; then strain through a medium-fine strainer and add to the rest of the soup.

4. Sauté the croutons with the butter and spring onion and serve them with the hot soup, flavouring it with a dribbling of extra-virgin olive oil and freshly ground black pepper.

In winter this first course is truly excellent served piping hot. In summer it can be served luke-warm or cold, with a little basil pesto.

In the glass: suggested wines

The sommelier Mototsugu Hayashi suggests: Petite Arvine – Vigne Champorette – Les Crétes (Valle d'Aosta); Arbis Blanc – Borgo San Daniele (Friuli Venezia Giulia); Sancerre – A. Mellot (Loire, France).

dal Pescatore

Mezzelune filled with pike with Belgrano cornmeal wafers and traditional balsamic vinegar from Modena

Ingredients

FOR THE FILLING
Onion 1
Small carrot 1
Celery 1 stalk
Small spring onion 1
Butter 1/4 cup
White wine 1/2 cup
Lemon juice 1 teaspoon
Filleted pike 1/3 lb
Salt
Pepper

FOR THE PASTA
Egg yolks 6
Flour 1 cup

Butter
Breadcrumbs
Belgrano cornmeal wafers
(for the recipe, see p. 102)
Traditional balsamic vinegar
from Modena a few drops

Time: **20'**
plus making of the pasta

Preparation

1. In a copper pan, lightly sauté in butter a mixture of chopped onions, celery, carrots and spring onion; dampen with white wine and add the lemon juice.

2. For the filling, place in the pan the previously salted and peppered fillets of pike. Cook well for 8-10 minutes over moderate heat, so as to thicken the pan juices, then blend. Set aside to cool at room temperature.

3. For the pasta, add the egg yolks to the flour and work well to form a smooth, even dough. Roll the dough to a rectangular shape 1/16"-1\8" mm thick. Using a teaspoon, place little heaps of the filling on the dough, evenly spaced. Cover with a layer of pasta, press down around the heaps of filling, and cut in the preferred shape (mezzaluna, tortelli, ravioli).

4. Cook the mezzelune in boiling salted water for 3 minutes.

5. Dress with butter and breadcrumbs and serve with small leaves of polenta and traditional balsamic vinegar from Modena.

In preparing the filling, be very careful to remove all bones from the pike. If this fish is not readily available, you can use the same recipe with turbo.

In the glass: suggested wines

For this dish, we suggest a classic Trebbiano d'Abruzzo (from Masciarelli or Valentini); another excellent accompaniment is Verdicchio del Castello di Jesi – Villa Bucci (Marche). Alternatively, you can choose a French wine, such as Meursault Perrières – J.F. Coche-Dury (Bourgogne, France) or a Riesling Leon Beyer (Alsace, France).

Potato gnocchi with cherry tomatoes, basil and extra-virgin olive oil from Abruzzo

Ingredients

Potatoes 1/2 lb
Flour 2/3 cup
Cherry tomatoes 1/2 cup
Basil
Extra-virgin olive oil from Abruzzo
Salt
Pepper

Time: 35'

Preparation

1. Put the potatoes, unpeeled, into a pot of cold salted water; boil until done, peel and mash them on a cutting board.

2. Add the flour to the mashed potatoes, mixing to form a dough that does not stick to the hands (the more flour you use, the harder the gnocchi will be when cooked).

3. Divide the dough into pieces, forming small rolls; cut the rolls into bite-size pieces.

4. Plunge the gnocchi into boiling salted water and cook until they rise to the surface.

5. Serve them with fresh tomatoes and basil in flower, blended with a dribbling of extra-virgin olive oil from Abruzzo and freshly ground black pepper.

Gnocchi are a dish that everyone likes, children in particular. They are also easy and fun to prepare; let one of your children help you. It will be a very pleasant occasion for both of you.

In the glass: suggested wines

Alto Adige Bianco Beyond The Clouds – E. Walch (Alto Adige); Sauvignon – B. Brandolini d'Adda (Friuli Venezia Giulia); Petite Arvine Vigne Champorette – Les Crétes (Val d'Aosta); Champagne Brut – Bonnaire (Champagne, France); Franciacorta Satèn – Magnificentia Uberti (Lombardy).

Second courses

A DIGRESSION ON SECOND COURSES that covers every aspect of our cuisine: the products of our territory, such as carp, and the products of traditional peasant cooking, such as pork; but also fine seafood and bluefish. Therefore varied raw materials, and the demonstration that our work consists of details that make the difference: how to choose the right wine to accompany a certain dish. At the restaurant, wine has a special role, sharing the spotlight with the dish it accompanies, guaranteeing the harmony of the meal. Everything has a significance of its own: the colour, the fragrance, the bottle, the serving temperature (45 °F/7 °C for Champagne, 50-60 °F/11-16 °C for white wines, 60-62 °F/16-17 °C for reds, and 53-60 °F/12-16 °C for fortified wines). An exceptional fount of messages, wine must speak of the land that produced it, to evoke authentic emotions. Today the consumer is better informed; but as declares Jean Siegrist, professor at the Institut Oenologique de Beaune, to understand a wine you must train your taste, using methodology and technical rigour.

Braised guineafowl with peaches

Ingredients

Breasts of guineafowl 2
Shallot 1
Stalk of celery 1
Sliced ripe peaches 2
Butter 1/3 cup
Rosemary 1 twig
Lemon 1/2
White wine 1/4 cup
Stock 1/2 cup
Madeira 1 tablespoon

Time: **20'**

Preparation

1. Finely chop the shallot with the celery. In a non-stick pan, sauté these ingredients in butter; when they start to brown, add the white wine and simmer.

2. Remove the vegetables and the aromatised liquid from the pan and set aside. In the same pan, brown the breasts of guineafowl with the rosemary over moderate heat, turning them constantly to form an even crust.

3. Add a little at a time the aromatised liquid, the stock, the peaches and lastly the Madeira. Cook for about 1 minute, then remove the guineafowl breasts from the pan and keep them warm.

4. Strain the cooking liquid and reduce it to the ideal density.

5. Slice the guineafowl breasts and serve them with the sauce, the peaches and seasonal vegetables.

In the glass: suggested wines

Vistamare – Gaja (Tuscany); Sylvaner – Abbazia di Novacella (Trentino-Alto Adige); Cerasuolo D'Abruzzo – Valentini (Abruzzo); Gewürztraminer Grand Cru Osterberg, Kientzler (Alsace, France).

Lièvre à la Royale

Ingredients (serves 8-10)

Hare 1
Sliced fillet of pork 3 1/2 oz
Sliced bacon 3 1/2 oz
Day-old bread 1/2 cup
Garlic without the bud, fresh thyme, sage and rosemary chopped together 1 clove
Foie gras 7 oz
Black truffles 1 2/3 oz
Egg 1 (or 2 for a very large hare)
Marc de Bourgogne or Brandy 3 tablespoons

FOR THE MARINADE
Carrots 2
Onions 2
Shallots 4
Bouquet of celery, parsley, thyme and bay leaf
Salt
White pepper
Structured red wine 4 quarts
Reinette apples 2

Extra-virgin olive oil 3 tablespoons
Honey 1 tablespoon
Butter 1/4 cup

Time: 6h
plus marinade

Preparation

1. Clean the hare, conserving the liver and heart.
Remove the bones entirely, trying not to pierce the skin.
Place all of the vegetables for the marinade in large bowl together with the bones of the hare. Add the red wine, the apples cut in pieces and lastly the deboned hare. Marinate for 24 hours.

2. For the filling, break the bread into pieces, place them in a bowl and add the Marc de Bourgogne or Brandy, then add the sliced fillet of pork, the mixture of chopped aromatic herbs and garlic, the foie gras, the liver and heart of the hare and lastly the egg. Mix well.

3. Arrange the slices of bacon, one beside another, on a large sheet of oven paper to form a base on which to place the hare, well open. Flavour with salt and pepper, then place the filling and the sliced truffles in the middle.

4. With the aid of the oven paper, close the hare, pressing the slices of bacon around it; tie it with several turns of butcher's twine.

5. Brown the stuffed hare with olive oil and butter in a deep pan until crusty all over. Add the marinade with the bones and vegetables, cover and simmer for 4-5 hours over low heat.

6. When the hare is done, remove it from the pan, strain the pan juices, add the honey and reduce the sauce.
Serve the stuffed hare, cut in thick slices, with the red wine sauce.

In the glass: suggested wines

Vin Clos de L'Ermitage – Jean Alesi (Rhône, France); Barolo riserva "Vigna Madonna Assunta La Villa" – Podere Rocche dei Manzoni; Sorì Tildin – Gaja (Piemonte); Sassicaia – Tenuta San Guido (Tuscany); Gevrey- Chambertin Lavaut Saint-Jacques – Denis Mortet (Burgundy, France); Amarone della Valpolicella – Allegrini (Veneto).

Gurnard in cartouche with vegetables, Pachino tomatoes, Taggiasche olives and Tuscan or Umbrian extra-virgin olive oil

Ingredients

Gurnard (2-4 lbs) 1
Tropea onions
Carrots
Celery
Aubergine
Pachino tomatoes
Taggiasche olives
Extra-virgin Tuscan or Umbrian olive oil 8 1/2 tablespoons
White wine 2 1/2 tablespoons
Garlic 1 clove
Basil leaves
Thyme
Rock salt
Pepper

Time: 40'

Preparation

1. In a large aluminium pan, heat 6 1/2 tablespoons of olive oil with the garlic; add the cubed vegetables, stir and cook until crunchy. Then add the white wine and the olives, the pepper, salt and basil leaves.

2. In the meantime, place a large sheet of aluminium foil in a fish-kettle. Oil the aluminium foil with 2 1/2 tablespoons of olive oil, then place on it the fish with all of the lightly wilted vegetables. Add the tomatoes and thyme; close the sheet of aluminium foil well and bake at 345-350 °F/175-180 °C for at least 25 minutes (you can check for doneness using a skewer: the fish is done when the skewer passes through it from one side to the other easily).

3. Remove from the oven and serve accompanied by all of the vegetables.

Since this recipe reveals the freshness of the fish, intensifying its flavour, it calls for a product of the highest quality.

In the glass: suggested wines

For this dish, the sommelier Mototsugu Hayashi has selected the following wines: Lugana Riserva – Zenato (Veneto); Trebbiano d'Abruzzo Marina Cvetic – Masciarelli (Abruzzo); Stalk d'Amalfi Furore Bianco Fiorduva – M. Cuomo (Campania); Vintage Tunina – Jermann (Friuli Venezia Giulia).

Sea bass and lobster pan-cooked with garden herbs, asparagus tips and vegetables

Ingredients

Sea bass (1 1/3 lbs) 1
Lobster 1
Spring onion
Hearts of green celery
Carrots
Green asparagus
Fennel
Tuscan extra-virgin olive oil 3 tablespoons
Garlic 1 clove
Rind of Sorrento lemon
Basil
Meat stock
White wine 2 tablespoons

Rounds of toasted bread (optional)
Chili pepper (optional)

Time: **10'**

Preparation

1. Fillet the bass and heat. In an aluminium pan, heat 2 1/2 tablespoons of extra-virgin olive oil and the unpeeled garlic. When the oil is hot, add the fillets and cook over moderate heat for 30 seconds.

2. Then add the vegetables and the hot stock.

3. Cook the fish carefully, turning it delicately. Add the wine, and lastly the basil leaves and lemon rind.

4. Plunge the lobster into boiling water for one minute, then remove the flesh from the shell in 4 portions. Add the lobster to the sea bass only after having removed the pan from the heat. Flavour with 3/4 tablespoon of savoury Tuscan extra-virgin olive oil.

5. Serve the hot dish immediately. If you wish, you can accompany it with crunchy rounds of toasted bread, and add a little chili pepper.

For this recipe we have chosen fine fish and seafood which are, for their characteristics, the height of refinement. Be sure, however, to choose fish caught in the sea and not produced in fish farms.

In the glass: suggested wines

For this sublime second course we suggest an intensely fragrant white wine, such as: Friuli Isonzo Chardonnay – Vie di Romans (Friuli Venezia Giulia); Sauvignon – Lageder (Alto Adige). Other perfect accompaniments are: Champagne Brut – Bonnaire (Champagne, France); Franciacorta Satèn – Ca' del Bosco (Lombardy).

dal Pescatore
Santini

Fried carp and eels

Ingredients

Fresh-water carp 3/4 - 1 lb
Eels from Lake Garda or the Mincio 1/2 lb
Ligurian extra-virgin olive oil
Rock salt
Spring onion
Garden radicchio
Vinegar
Salt

Time: 30'

Preparation

1. Clean the carp and the eels and wash them thoroughly.

2. Place them on kitchen paper and sprinkle with rock salt to make the skin crunchy.

3. Heat the extra-virgin olive oil in a pan; when it is sizzling hot, add the eel cut into small strips and the carp cut into slices. Fry until golden brown and crunchy.

4. Serve with the spring onion and the garden radicchio, sliced fine and dressed with olive oil, vinegar and salt.

A simple but tasty recipe; like eels, in fact, freshwater carp is excellent served just fried.

In the glass: suggested wines

Sauvignon – Brandolini d'Adda (Friuli Venezia Giulia); Collio Pinot Bianco – Villa Russiz (Friuli Venezia Giulia); Capitel Croce – R. Anselmi (Veneto); Brut Riserva Elena – Podere Rocche dei Manzoni (Piemonte); Champagne Brut – Bonnaire (Champagne, France).

Dentex with white Sorana beans and Tuscan extra-virgin olive oil

Ingredients

Dentex 4 thick slices
White Sorana beans, fresh or dried and soaked in cold water for at least 12 hours
Bay leaf 1
Carrot 1
Green celery 1 stalk
Shallot 1
Tropea onion 1
Vegetable or meat stock 2 and 1/2 ladles
Whole black pepper
Tuscan extra-virgin olive oil

Time: 35'
plus soaking of the beans

Preparation

1. Put the beans in a pot, cover with water and add a few grains of pepper and the bay leaf. Simmer slowly for 20 minutes, adding a few drops of extra-virgin olive oil.

2. In a separate pot, place the cold stock, a carrot, a small stalk of green celery, the shallot and the onion.

3. Immerse the fish in the stock and heat to medium temperature. When a little steam begins to form, remove the pot from the heat and let it cool slightly.

4. Serve the dentex warm, together with the beans, flavouring it with Tuscan extra-virgin olive oil and, if you like, freshly ground black pepper.

Dentex is a fish that goes perfectly with Sorana beans, in a recipe that is both simple and refined.

In the glass: suggested wines

Alto Adige Chardonnay Cornell – Produttori di Colterenzio (Alto Adige); Verdicchio Classico dei Castelli di Jesi – Villa Bucci (Marche); Pouilly-Fumé Pur Sang – D. Dagueneau (Loire, France); Chardonnay – R. Mondavi (California).

Grilled eel

Ingredients (serves 2)

Eel (1 2/3 lbs) 1
Fennel 1/2
Celery 1 stalk
Butter 1 1/2 tablespoons
Dried bay leaves
Rosemary
Garlic 1 clove

Time: **20'**

Preparation

1. Clean and scale the eel, if possible without breaking the skin.

2. Cut the eel into portions, place them in a pot of cold salted water and cook them along with the fennel and celery, which will cause the eel to lose much of its fat.

3. Bring the water to a boil, then remove the pieces of eel with a skimmer.

4. In a skillet, sauté the eel with a little butter, the rosemary and the bay leaves until a fine crust forms on it.

5. Finish cooking the eel under the grill, first with the skin side up, then carefully turning it.

6. You can also cook the eel in large pieces, directly in a non-stick pan with butter, rosemary and garlic (1 unpeeled clove) and the dried bay leaves. In this case, it should cook very slowly. The very low heat will cause the fat in the skin to melt, leaving it tender and crunchy, done to perfection.

Eels, tench, carp and catfish live in rivers and lakes. The best quality can be recognised by the colour of the belly, which should be a pronounced yellow-green. This is the only way to be sure that the fish has lived in the cleanest running water.

In the glass: suggested wines

This dish goes perfectly with a white wine or a red one with a good degree of acidity such as: Friulano Collio– Schiopetto (Friuli Venezia Giulia); Chardonnay Cuvée Bois – Les Crêtes (Valle d'Aosta); Riesling Clos Sainte-Hune – Trimbach (Alsace, France). Another excellent choice is Cerasuolo d'Abruzzo – Valentini (Abruzzo).

Pan-cooked carp (Grandma Teresa's recipe)

Ingredients

Carp (about 2 lbs) 1
Onions 2
Celery 2 stalks
Carrot 2
Anchovies 2
Tomato sauce 7 tablespoons
Extra-virgin olive oil
Stock 2 ladles
Salt
Pepper

Peas

Time: 45'

Preparation

1. Clean and wash the carp, then simmer it in a pot of water in order to remove the backbone.

2. Chop the vegetables and anchovies very fine; add 4 tablespoons of tomato sauce. Stuff the fish with this mixture.

3. Cover the bottom of a pan with a thin layer of extra-virgin olive oil, add 3 tablespoons of tomato sauce, salt and pepper, then place the carp in the pan.

4. Simmer over low heat for about 30 minutes, adding 2 ladles of stock to keep the pan juices from drying out. When the fish is done, divide it into portions and serve together with the sauce.

This classic of our cuisine is not always available, since procuring a carp, a fish that is either loved or detested, is not a simple matter today. But if you are lucky enough to taste it, you will discover that it contains a world of authentic flavours evoking rivers and lakes, and emitting the fragrance of the land and the herbs of our territory. In springtime you can enhance the presentation of this dish by accompanying it with fresh peas from the garden, as we have done.

In the glass: suggested wines

Perfect accompaniments are Chiaretto del Lago di Garda (Veneto) or a Bardolino Chiaretto (Veneto); with this dish you can also sample a Trebbiano d'Abruzzo – Valentini (Abruzzo), authentic and potent, or a Chardonnay – Planeta (Sicily). Alternatively, you can choose a Coulée de Serrant – Joly (Loire, France) or a classic Meursault Les Rougeots – J.F. Coche-Dury (Bourgogne, France).

Fresh cod in a terracotta pot, yellow polenta with soup (onions, garlic, anchovies and milk)

Ingredients

Fresh cod 1 lbs
Finely chopped onions 2/3 cup
Extra-virgin olive oil 5 tablespoons
Anchovies preserved in salt 2
Chopped fresh parsley 1 tablespoon
Garlic 1 clove
Stock 1 ladle
Milk 5 tablespoons
Grated Parmesan 1 1/4 tablespoons
Flour 1/2 cup
Yellow cornmeal quenelles

Time: 45'

Preparation

1. Heat the extra-virgin olive oil in a terracotta pot. Add the finely chopped white onion; cook and stir over low heat for 5 minutes.

2. Cut the cod into pieces, roll them in the flour and the grated Parmesan; place them delicately in the terracotta pot and cover with a mixture of finely chopped anchovies, previously washed and deboned, parsley, garlic, milk and stock.

3. Simmer for about 20 minutes and serve with yellow cornmeal quenelles.

This dish is a variation of the classic "Baccalà alla vicentina" (Vicenza-style cod). It is usually accompanied with freshly-made yellow or white cornmeal polenta.

In the glass: suggested wines

Colli Orientali del Friuli Ronco delle Acace – Le Vigne di Zamò (Friuli Venezia Giulia); Colli di Luni Vermentino Boboli – Giacomelli (Liguria); Franciacorta Brut Cobochon (Lombardy); Franciacorta Brut Cuvée Pas operé – Bellavista (Lombardy); Franciacorta Sublimis – Uberti (Lombardy); Pouilly-Fumé Pur Sang – D. Dagueneau (Loire, France).

Baked stuffed tench

Ingredients

Tench 1 1/2 lbs
Fennel 1
Lemon juice 1
Salt

FOR THE STUFFING
Bread 1 cup
Chopped amaretti 2 1/2 tablespoons
Grated Parmesan 1 tablespoon
Anchovy 1/2

Butter 2 tablespoons
Grated lemon rind
Meat stock
Sage a few leaves
Rosemary 1 twig
Extra-virgin olive oil
Salt
Pepper

Time: 35'

Preparation

1. Clean and wash the tench. Simmer it in a pan with water, fennel, salt and lemon juice for about 10 minutes, then cool. When cold, remove the backbone, opening the fish lengthwise.

2. In the meantime, prepare the stuffing by mixing in a large, deep bowl the bread, amaretti, grated Parmesan and anchovy. Add the boiling-hot stock and mix well to amalgamate all of the ingredients.

3. Stuff the two halves of the fish, adding salt, pepper, lemon rind, oil, a few leaves of sage and rosemary and a few curls of butter.

4. Bake at 300 °F/150 °C for 10-15 minutes. Remove from the oven and serve.

Tench is a fish commonly found in the lakes of Lombardy. This recipe thus has ancient roots. The presence of Parmesan, just as in "Baccalà alla vicentina", reveals in fact flavours and combinations sanctioned by tradition, but well balanced and highly appreciated today as well.

In the glass: suggested wines

Franciacorta Brut Annamaria Clementi – Ca' del Bosco (Lombardy); Brut Cuvée Louise Pommery (Champagne, France); Alteni di Brassica – Gaja (Piemonte); Trento Doc Riserva Giulio Ferrari (Trentino).

Turbo with extra-virgin olive oil from Lake Garda, parsley, anchovies and Salina capers

Ingredients

Turbo (about 1/3 lb each) 4
Lemon 1/2
Celery 1 stalk
Fennel 1/2
Salt
Water

FOR THE SAUCE
Parsley 2 handfuls
Salina capers 1 teaspoon
Garlic 1 clove
Anchovy 1/2
Extra-virgin olive oil from Lake Garda

Toasted polenta
Radicchio

Time: 15'

Preparation

1. Place the fish in a large pan, cover with cold water and add the celery and fennel. Salt and heat to boiling point, then remove from the heat and let cool to luke-warm. In the meantime prepare the sauce.

2. For the sauce, place in a pan the chopped parsley and capers, the finely chopped garlic and the minced anchovy. Cover with olive oil and heat. Bring to boiling point, remove the sauce from the heat and pour it into a sauce-boat to stop the cooking process and keep the parsley bright green.

3. Remove the fish from the water and serve it with the sauce, the toasted polenta and finely sliced green radicchio.

Pike too is often cooked in this way. Because of its characteristic forked bones, cook it in a fish-kettle with cold water, adding half an onion, a stalk of celery, a pinch of salt and some peppercorns. As soon as steam begins to form, remove from the heat and stop the cooking process by placing the fish-kettle on a cold surface. After at least 10 minutes, pick up the fish in your hands to be sure that the flesh detaches from the bones easily.

In the glass: suggested wines

The wines to accompany this dish are recommended by my friend Tano Martini from the legendary restaurant Il Cigno in Mantua, who, together with Roberto Ferrari of the famous Il Bersagliere di Goito (whose precious advice we have used for another recipe) is one of the finest sommeliers in the AIS. With the turbot, Tano suggests: Sauvignon la Prendina – Piona (Lombardy); Ribolla Gialla – Puiatti (Friuli Venezia Giulia); Bianco di Custoza – Corte Gardoni (Veneto); Pouilly-Fumé Baron de Ladoucette (Loire, France).

dal Pescatore
Santini

Frog legs with fine herbs au gratin

Ingredients (serves 2)

Extra-fresh frog legs 10
Butter 1/2 cup
Garlic 1 clove
Chopped parsley 1 tablespoon
Breadcrumbs 1 cup
Whole eggs 1
Egg white 1
Salt
Pepper

Time: 40'
plus cleaning of the frogs

Preparation

1. Gut and skin the frogs; using sharp, pointed scissors, cut off the lower thighs and, with the point, remove the bone from each thigh.

2. In a deep round bowl, beat the whole egg and the egg white together with a fork, add salt and pepper; dip the frog legs in the beaten egg mixture, then coat them with breadcrumbs.

3. In a large non-stick pan, melt the butter with the clove of garlic cut in half. Then add the frog legs, turning them gently to brown evenly on all sides.

4. Remove the frog legs and add to the butter in the pan a tablespoon of breadcrumbs and a pinch of very finely chopped parsley.

5. Place the frog legs on a serving dish and dress them with this tasty parsley sauce.

Use Italian frogs of medium size, considering portions of 10 legs (that is, 5 frogs) for each guest. Do not throw away any leftovers. With the rest of the meat, you can make a good soup or an excellent risotto.

In the glass: suggested wines

This second course calls for a white wine of character, either still or sparkling, such as a spumante or a Champagne. Our choices are: Trebbiano d'Abruzzo Marina Cvetic – Masciarelli (Abruzzo); Where the Dreams Chardonnay – Jermann (Friuli Venezia Giulia); Franciacorta Brut Collezione Cavalleri (Lombardy); Comte de Champagne Blanc des Blancs – Taittinger (Champagne, France); Ridge Chardonnay Santa Cruz Mountains (California).

Pork liver and loin with caul fat and onions

Ingredients

Pork liver (or fillet of pork) 3/4 lb
Liver caul 1 oz
Butter 1/3 cup
Pork loin 1/2 lb
Onion 1 small
Rosemary 1 twig
Sage
Lemon 1/2
White wine 1 tablespoon
Salt
Pepper

FOR THE POLENTA
Water 4 ladles
Whole-grain cornmeal 1 cup
Salt 1 pinch
Extra-virgin olive oil 1 tablespoon
Butter 1 3/4 tablespoons

Time: 30'

Preparation

1. In a copper pan, melt the butter over low heat. Add the sliced onion and brown lightly.

2. Cut the caul into pieces and add it to the sautéd onion; add the sliced pork loin (or fillet, if you prefer). Stir well with a wooden spatula and add the liver, sage and rosemary; salt and pepper. Add the white wine, let it evaporate and lastly the lemon juice.

3. On very low heat, simmer until the meat is tender and the liver crunchy and well browned.

4. For the polenta, heat the water, salt and extra-virgin olive oil in an aluminium pot. When the water starts to boil, sprinkle the cornmeal into it until it is about as thick as boiled custard, stirring constantly with a wire whisk. Continue stirring, using a wooden spoon or spatula, until the polenta begins to detach from the walls of the pot. Pour it onto a cutting board and let it cool.

5. Cut the cold polenta into pieces and sauté them in non-stick pan with the butter to form a golden crust. Add the pieces of polenta to the mixture and let them absorb the flavours for a few minutes.

6. Arrange the pieces of liver on plates and serve with the fried polenta.

This recipe has the savour of an ancient rite, that of slaughtering the pig, which involved a farmer's whole family in the past. For dinner they ate the liver and loin cooked just in this way; but it was a privilege reserved exclusively to those who had participated in the event.

IN THE GLASS: SUGGESTED WINES

Maurizio Zanella – Ca' del Bosco (Lombardy); Sassicaia – Marchese Incisa della Rocchetta (Tuscany); Siepi – Castello di Fonterutoli (Tuscany); Solaia – P. Antinori (Tuscany); Sfursat 5 Stelle – Negri (Lombardy); Sagrantino di Montefalco 25 anni – A. Caprai (Umbria); Messorio – Le Macchiole (Tuscany); Château Musar – G. Hoscar (Bekaa, Lebanon).

Liver with onions and polenta Venetian style

Ingredients

Veal liver 4 slices
Butter 1/4 cup
Sage
Rosemary
Stock 2 ladles
Spring onions 2
Breadcrumbs 1 1/3 cups
Salt and pepper

Polenta

Time: **10'**

Preparation

1. In a large teflon pan, melt the butter over moderate heat; add the thinly sliced spring onions, cover with stock and simmer.

2. Meanwhile, coat the slices of liver in the breadcrumbs, add them to the pan and turn them several times, being careful not to let them toughen; flavour with sage and rosemary. Taste for salt and pepper.

3. Serve with hot polenta (see recipe on page 172).

A classic of the Veneto tradition seen through Lombard eyes, a simple recipe that exalts the unique range of flavours of liver, whose taste harmonizes perfectly with the sweetish note of the onion.

In the glass: suggested wines

Valpolicella – Quintarelli (Veneto), Barbera d'Asti – Scarpa (Piemonte); San Leonardo – Guerrieri Gonzaga (Trentino); Granato – Foradori (Trentino); Bolgheri Rosso Superiore – Guado al Tasso (Tuscany); Franciacorta Brut Riserva – Ca' del Bosco (Lombardy); Penfold Shiraz – Rwt Penfolds (Barossa Valley, Australia).

Baked or grilled chicken "alla diavola"

Ingredients (serves 4-6)

FOR THE BAKED CHICKEN
Cockerel (about 4 lbs) 1
Extra-virgin olive oil 1/2 cup
Lemon (juice of) 1
Rosemary 1 twig
Stock 2 ladles
White wine 1/2 cup
Salt
Pepper

FOR THE GRILLED CHICKEN
Cockerel (about 4 lbs) 1
Garlic 2 cloves
Chopped parsley 1 tablespoon
Vinegar 1 tablespoon
Lemon (juice of) 1
Extra-virgin olive oil 6 1/2 tablespoons
Salt
Pepper

FOR THE PARSLEY SAUCE
Chopped parsley 2 tablespoons
Garlic 1/2 clove
Extra-virgin olive oil
Vinegar 1 teaspoon
Lemon (juice of) 1/2
Salt and pepper

Time:
the preparation time varies depending on the chicken breed, and on the way the chicken was raised

Preparation

Baked chicken:
1. Cut the chicken into pieces and arrange them in a lasagne pan.

2. In a bowl, mix the oil and lemon juice; salt and pepper. Beat well with a wire whisk and pour over the pieces of chicken. Add the stock, the wine and the rosemary.

3. Place in an unheated oven and set the temperature at 345 °F/175 °C. Bake, turning the pieces until well browned on all sides, for at least 45 minutes. Serve piping hot.

Grilled chicken:
1. Cut the chicken into pieces, leaving them to marinate for 12 hours in a large glass bowl with the crushed garlic, the oil, vinegar and lemon juice. Add abundant pepper and salt and lastly add the chopped parsley. Stir well to marinate and flavour the meat, which will be more tender and appetising. Place the bowl in the least cold part of the refrigerator.

2. Grill the meat over hot coals on a barbecue pit. Grill the chicken until it is golden brown with a crunchy crust. The secret consists in keeping the hot charcoal at a certain distance; it will take longer to cook, but will cook better and more evenly.

Parsley sauce:
Place the parsley in a bowl, add the garlic and cover with olive oil, vinegar and lemon juice; add salt and pepper. Mix well and serve at once, with the baked or grilled chicken.

For these two classics we use cockerels raised by Luciano Pigorini. A simple secret is the parsley sauce, which goes very well with roasts and meat cooked on a skewer. This recipe for grilled cockerel can also be used to cook lamb chops and pork sausage.

In the glass: suggested wines

Barbaresco Asili – B. Giocosa (Piemonte); Pergole Torte – Montevertine (Tuscany); Sperss Nebbiolo – Gaja (Piemonte); Barolo Cannubi – E. Pira e figli (Piemonte); Sodi di San Nicolò – Castellare (Tuscany); Sélection Côtes du Rhône Mon Coeur – J.L. Chave (Côtes du Rhône, France).

Saddle of venison with Cabernet sauce

Ingredients

Saddle of venison 1 3/4 lbs
Red wine 2 cups
Butter 1/3 cup
Celery 1 stalk
Carrot 1
Onion 1
Pepper 2 pinches
Sale 1 pinch
Nutmeg 1 pinch
Cloves
Rosemary 1 twig
White wine 1/2 cup
Beef stock 2 ladles
Acacia honey 1 teaspoon
Blueberries

Seasonable vegetables

Time: **20'**
plus marinade

Preparation

1. Debone the saddle of venison, break the bones into pieces and set them aside. Marinate the meat for 1 and 1/2 hours in the red wine flavoured with the finely sliced celery, carrot and onion. Add salt, pepper and all of the spices.

2. Sauté the pieces of bone in 1/4 cup of butter, then add the wine used as marinade and all of the vegetables. Add a twig of rosemary and cover with a lid. Simmer to reduce the liquid and concentrate the flavour until the sauce is dense; strain it and set it aside.

3. Heat 2 tablespoons of butter in a pan and sauté the venison; add the white wine, salt and pepper. Simmer over low heat, turning the meat until it is evenly browned.
Add the rosemary; when the meat is done, remove it from the heat, keeping it warm for a few minutes. Add the beef stock to the pan and let it evaporate well so that the aroma of the venison, which has been slowly concentrating in the pan juices, thickens to a light sauce. Add the thick sauce formed by cooking the marinated bones.

4. When the sauce has thickened, strain it and taste for flavour; if it is very strong, add a teaspoon of acacia honey and some blueberries.

5. Serve the venison with seasonal vegetables.

The success of this dish depends basically on the meat, which should be hung but not too long, and should remain pink after cooking. A little secret for its presentation: before arranging the saddle of venison on a serving platter, pour a generous portion of the sauce onto the platter. This will enhance the pink colour of the meat.

In the glass: suggested wines

Barolo Riserva 7 anni – Podere Rocche dei Manzoni (Piemonte); Camp Gros Barbaresco – Marchesi di Gresy (Piemonte); Barbaresco Vigneto Gallina – La Spinetta (Piemonte); Sassicaia – Marchese Incisa della Rocchetta (Tuscany); Pinot Noir Sonoma Coast Kanzler Vineyard – Kosta Browne (California); Chambertin – D. Laurent (Bourgogne, France); Grand Échézeaux – Dom. de la Romanée-Conti (Bourgogne, France).

Sirloin steak (Chianina) with aromatic herbs

Ingredients (serves 4-6)

Sirloin steak (Chianina, the roast-beef cut) 1 3/4 lbs
Spiced Colonnata lard 2 tablespoons
Extra-virgin olive oil
Juniper berries 10-12
Rosemary 1 twig
Sugar 1 pinch
Stock 1 1/2 ladles
Top-quality red wine 1 cup
Mixed spices
Thyme
Marjoram
Mint
Rosemary 1 twig
Sage
Lemon rind 1
Salt
Pepper

Baked potatoes, buttered fennel, fried artichokes

Time: 20'

Preparation

1. Heat the olive oil in a tin-plated copper pan; when hot, add the meat and brown for at least 2 minutes. Then add the juniper berries and 1/2 twig of rosemary; salt and pepper.
Continue to brown the meat until crusty on the outside; on the sides and in the bottom of the pan, tiny particles of roast meat will have formed.

2. Remove the meat and add the stock to the pan juices; add the red wine and the mixed spices.

3. Continue cooking the meat in another pan, along with the olive oil and finely cut spiced lard; flavour with 1/2 twig of rosemary. When the sauce in the first pan thickens, check for quality: it should have a mellow, harmonious taste. At this point, strain it and pour it into a gravy-boat.

4. In the meantime the meat, which has been turned several times, will have become perfectly done. Remove it from the heat, chop fine all of the herbs and the lemon rind, and serve with baked potatoes, buttered fennel and fried artichokes.

A classic dish, irresistible to all lovers of red meat, enhanced by a mellow, tasty sauce. Absolutely to be tried with the wines suggested by the great Tonino Trimboli.

In the glass: suggested wines

With the Chianina sirloin steak, Tonino Trimboli combines a traditional wine such as a good Nebbiolo, a Bourgogne Premier Cru or the most classic of the Chianti Gallo Nero old-style wines, without the contribution of Cabernet. But he does not advise a great wine (a Barolo or a Chambertin) that could "cover" the taste of the dish. In alternative, he recommends accompanying it with a Bordeaux, not so much a Medoc as a Pomerol or a Saint Emilion. A final recommendation from this expert: the wine you use in cooking deserves to be as good as the dish to which it contributes gusto. It must be of good quality then; you can drink what is left over during the meal.

Pigeons roasted with lard flavoured with herbs and spices

Ingredients

Young pigeons 4
Arnad lard or bacon 4 slices
Cinnamon
Nutmeg
Cloves
Rosemary 1 twig
Sage 5 small leaves
Lemon juice 1
Cognac 2 tablespoons
Butter
Salt and pepper

FOR THE STUFFING:
Stock 4 cups
Breadcrumbs 1 tablespoon
Apple mostarda
Amaretto 1
Egg yolk or pigeon's egg 1
Salt and pepper

FOR THE POTATOES
Potatoes 1/2 cup
Butter 1/3 cup
Extra-virgin olive oil
Garlic 1 clove
Rosemary 1 twig
Pounded lard
Salt and pepper

Time: 45'

Preparation

1. Clean and singe the pigeons. Wash them well, dry and set aside.

2. For the stuffing, bring to a boil 4 cups of stock, add the breadcrumbs and mix well to form a mixture as thick as polenta; add the pepper, the chopped mostarda and the amaretto, broken into bits. Then add the egg yolk or pigeon's egg, stir well for a few minutes with a wooden spoon and stuff the pigeons.

3. Tie the legs of the pigeons together to keep the filling inside during cooking, then place them in a copper pot. Dress with the butter, pepper, salt, rosemary, sage and lemon juice; lastly, add a tablespoon of Cognac.

4. Brown well for at least 3 minutes.

5. Place extra-fresh slices of Arnad lard on the breast and thighs of the pigeons, along with all of the herbs and roast in an oven preheated to 340 °F/170 °C. Let the lard melt and check for doneness after at least 15 minutes. Strain the pan juices and thin them (that is, add a few tablespoons of beef stock and heat again, stirring to form a smooth, even sauce.

6. For the roasted potatoes, peel, wash and dry the potatoes and cut them in regular pieces. Put them in a non-stick pan with the butter, olive oil, garlic and rosemary. Brown them over low heat, stirring frequently. Add salt and pepper; when half cooked (about 10 minutes) add a few pieces of pounded lard.

7. Serve the pigeons with the roasted potatoes.

You can also serve this dish with baked potatoes or roasted vegetables.

In the glass: suggested wines

Barolo – Voerzio, aged at least 8 years (Piemonte); Montruc Barbera d'Asti – Martinetti (Piemonte); San Leonardo – Guerrieri Gonzaga (Trentino); Clos de l'Hermitage Côte du Rhône – H. de Lanzac, J. Alesi (Côte du Rhône, France); Shiraz Carnival of Love – Mollydooker (McLaren Vale, Australia).

Suckling pig (Cinta Senese) with Sechuan peppercorns, caramelised pineapple, braised Savoy cabbage and red turnip sherbet

Ingredients

Shoulder or ribs of suckling pig (Cinta Senese) 30 oz
Water to cover
Butter 1/4 cup
Dry white wine 2 1/2 tablespoons
Italian brandy 1 1/2 tablespoons
Rosemary 1 twig
Sage a few leaves
Lemon (juice of) 1
Beef stock 3 ladles
Celery 1 small stalk
Sliced green onion 1
Sechuan pepper or black peppercorns
Salt and pepper

FOR THE PINEAPPLE
Pineapple 8 wedges
Butter
Stock 1 tablespoon

FOR THE CABBAGE
Savoy cabbage 1
Olive oil
Spiced lard 1 slice

Time: 20'

Preparation

1. Place the meat in a large pan and add the butter, juice of 1/2 lemon, celery, green onion, sage, rosemary, white wine, brandy and stock; salt and pepper.

2. Cover with water and simmer over medium heat for about 40 minutes, until all of the water has evaporated. The meat will be tender and the pan juices creamy. Strain and place in a pan.

3. Roast the meat in an oven preheated to 350-400 °F/180-200 °C for 10 minutes, to let the skin brown and become crunchy. Otherwise, put the meat in a non-stick pan with a tablespoon of pan juices until a crust forms (this will take 5-8 minutes).

4. In the meantime, prepare the pineapple and the cabbage. Cut the pineapple wedges into cubes 1/3" thick. Brown them in butter, add the stock and let cook until dry and crunchy. Blanche the cabbage in boiling water for a few minutes, sauté it in a little olive oil and flavour it with a slice of spiced lard.

5. Heat the strained pan juices, add the peppercorns, a little freshly ground pepper and the rest of the lemon juice, to flavour the dish and make it tastier.

6. Serve the suckling pig very hot, with the pan juices just off the heat, the cubes of crunchy pineapple and the sautéd cabbage.

For many years we have been using suckling pigs raised in Tuscany by Paolo Parisi, and we are truly grateful to him for the quality he has always been able to supply us with. In summer you can serve this dish with a red turnip sherbet.

In the glass: suggested wines

Barbaresco Rabaja – B. Giacosa (Piemonte); Promofine – Quintarelli (Veneto); Castello di Fonterutoli – Siepi (Tuscany); San Callisto Valle Reale – Ornellaia (Tuscany); Barolo Carobric – P. Scavino (Piemonte); Clos des Papes – Châteauneuf-du-Pape (Rhône Meridional, France).

KID RIBS WITH LEMON THYME SAUCE

Ingredients (serves 4-6)

Loin (with its ribs) 1
Whole shoulder 1
Garlic 2 cloves
Butter 1/4 cup
Rosemary 1 twig
Stock 3 ladles
White wine 2/3 cup
Extra-virgin olive oil 2 tablespoons
Cognac 2 tablespoons
Lemon juice 1
Lemon thyme 3 twigs
Salt
Pepper

Time: 35'

Preparation

1. In a copper pan, heat 2 tablespoons of olive oil, the garlic and the butter. When it begins to sizzle, add the meat along with the rosemary, salt and pepper.

2. Sauté over low heat until a golden crust forms on the meat and the pan juices taste good. The pan should be slightly "glazed". At this point, add the white wine, Cognac, stock and lemon juice. In a few minutes all of the liquid added will turn amber yellow.

3. Continue cooking, turning the pieces of meat frequently, for 4-5 minutes, then place in a very hot oven for 20-30 minutes. When done, the meat should be tender and pink.

4. Leave the dish to rest a little in the hot oven, adding the lemon thyme. Serve the meat very hot with its strained pan juices.

For cooking lamb ribs, I like to use a tin-plated copper or aluminium pan, since it guarantees perfect browning. In addition, the proteins from the meat are deposited on the sides of the pan and are toasted in contact with the metal. When I then add the white wine and stock, the gravy forms by itself with no need of flour.

IN THE GLASS: SUGGESTED WINES

Sori Tildin – Gaja (Piemonte); Chianti Montesodi – Frescobaldi (Tuscany); Saffredi – Fattoria Le Pupille (Tuscany); Pergole Torte – Montevertine (Tuscany); Deliella – Feudo Principi di Butera (Sicily); Cabernet Sauvignon Reserve – R. Mondavi (California).

Beef "Cappello da prete" with Barbera and Belgrano yellow polenta

Ingredients (serves 8)

Beef shoulder 2 lbs
Tropea red onions 1 lb
Celery 2 stalks
Carrots 2
Butter 3/4 cup
Red wine 8 cups
Finely sliced lard 1/4 lb
Rosemary
Sage 4 leaves
Salt
Pepper
Nutmeg 1 pinch
Cloves 1 pinch
Cinnamon 1 pinch

Beans
Toasted polenta

Time: 2h30'

Preparation

1. In a deep tin-plated copper or aluminium pan, sauté the vegetables in the butter and sliced lard for at least 10 minutes over low heat. When the vegetables are wilted, add the whole piece of meat and brown it well to form an even crust.

2. Only at this point, add enough wine to cover the meat abundantly, along with the rosemary and sage. Cover and simmer over low heat for 2 hours.

3. Use a fork to check for doneness. Remove the pot from the fire and pass the pan juices through a food mill, or blend with an immersion mixer, then strain through a fine strainer to form a smooth, even sauce.

4. Slice the meat when it has cooled to luke-warm and place the slices back in the sauce. Serve your dish with any kind of beans and with toasted polenta (see recipe on page 172).

The cut of meat chosen for this recipe is part of the front shoulder of the beef. Called "cappello da prete" in Milan and "pernice" in Mantua, it is unmistakeable for its characteristic veins of cartilage, which melt during cooking. A classic to bring to the table on cold, foggy winter days.

In the glass: suggested wines

Barbera d'Asti is the wine traditionally served with this dish: recommending it is almost obligatory. We suggest a Bricco dell'Uccellone – Braida (Piemonte) or a Montruc Barbera – Martinetti (Piemonte). You can also opt for a Barolo – Sandrone (Piemonte) or a great classic such as Barolo – B. Mascarello (Piemonte) or again, a Barolo – Rinaldi (Piemonte). In alternative, other magnificent combinations are both Barolo Monfortino – G. Conterno, aged 20 years (Piemonte) and precious Amarone, from Allegrini or Quintarelli (Veneto). Still more possible combinations are Opus One – Mondavi Rothschild (Red Napa Valley, California) and Vega Sicilia Unico – Bodegas Vega Sicilia (Ribera del Duero, Spain).

Stuffed hen

Ingredients

Hen (6 1/2 - 8 1/2 lbs) 1
Celery 1 stalk
Onion 1
Salt

FOR THE STUFFING
Breadcrumbs 1 1/3 cups
Amaretti 1/2 cup
Hen's liver
Eggs 2
Fruit mostarda 2 oz
Grated Parmesan 2/3 cup
Beef stock
Salt
Pepper

Fruit mostarda

Time: 2h30'
for free range hen there will be needed 4 hours at least

Preparation

1. For the stuffing, mix well all of the ingredients and add enough beef stock to ensure the right consistency.

2. Clean, wash and singe the hen. Stuff it, sew it together to keep the stuffing inside as it cooks, and tie it with butcher's twine.

3. In a large pot of water, place the hen along with the celery, onion and salt. Bring to a boil, skimming the pot if necessary.

4. Prick the hen under the wings several times as it cooks, to let the blood out and facilitate the cooking process.

5. Check for doneness by pressing a finger against the wingtips; when they have become very tender, the hen is done. Remove it from the heat and serve with the fruit mostarda and the stuffing.

Imagine a "virtual" trip through the fascinating world of sauces that accompany boiled meats: in France they use Dijon Mustard, in Piemonte a green sauce made of bread dampened in vinegar, hard-boiled eggs, anchovies, parsley, olive oil, pepper and a few capers. In Lombardy the most classic accompaniment is mashed potatoes, while in Milan they use fruit mostarda and in the Po Valley the stuffing of the hen. In Verona it is "pearà", a sauce made by boiling stock, breadcrumbs and a lot of pepper, that is usually served with boiled meats; in Vicenza and Trento, and then as far as Vienna, they prefer instead cren or horseradish.

In the glass: suggested wines

This great classic calls for an important wine, an aged red such as Barolo Gromis – Gaja (Piemonte) or a Brunello di Montalcino – Biondi Santi (Tuscany), or again a Brunello di Montalcino Riserva – Podere Brixio Bellini (Tuscany). It is also very good with an excellent wine from Central Italy: Sagrantino di Montefalco Riserva 25 years old – Caprai (Umbria).

Roast duck with Sicilian Tarocco orange sauce

Ingredients

Muscovy duck (4 - 4 1/2 lbs) 1
Butter 1/2 cup
Dry white wine 2 1/2 tablespoons
Meat or vegetable stock 7 ladles (about 3 cups)
Cognac 2 tablespoons
Juice of lemon 1
Tarocco oranges 2
Salt
Pepper
Rosemary 1 twig
Flour

Time: 1h30'
for domestic mallard 45 minutes will be enough

Preparation

1. After having cleaned, washed and singed the duck, place it breast up in a deep oven pan. Dot the meat with small pieces of butter, then sprinkle it with the wine and Cognac; add the pepper, salt, lemon juice and rosemary and pour over it evenly at least 3 cups of meat or vegetable stock.

2. Roast the duck in the oven preheated to a temperature of 340-355 °F/175-180 °C. Turn it repeatedly to ensure that it cooks evenly. The stock will evaporate slowly, leaving the meat tender and tasty. When the pan juices have reduced, the duck will be done. Remove it from the pan but keep it warm in the oven.

3. Slice one of the two oranges, squeeze it and add its juice to the pan juices.

4. Strain the pan juices, put the pan back over the heat and let the juices partially evaporate. Dust the orange slices lightly with flour and add them to the pan, to form a delicate sauce to be served with the duck.

5. To accompany the duck, braise the orange slices; to do this, put a few tablespoons of the pan juices in a pan, arrange the orange slices in it and set aside for an hour. Then heat the pan over low heat to keep the liquid from evaporating entirely. Lastly, serve the duck with the orange sauce.

This recipe, created in France or perhaps in Italy and imported there by the chefs of Caterina de' Medici, is by now a classic, found in the cuisine of many different countries. It is at its best when using a free-range duck. Our ducks, like our pullets, are supplied by the outstanding breeder from Piacenza, Luciano Pigorini.

In the glass: suggested wines

Duck with orange sauce has a predominant citrusy note, clearly evident to the taste. The wine chosen to go with it should balance this sensation. Hence the ideal is a red wine without too much body, fresh and fragrant, or a little more evolved but with no excessive tones. We suggest: Vistorta – Conti Brandolini d'Adda (Friuli Venezia Giulia); Promis Ca' Marcanda – A. Gaja (Tuscany); Pommard – J.F. Coche-Dury (Bourgogne, France).

Desserts

Grandma Bruna tells Alberto: "Every morning, on returning from the henhouse, Mamma Amabilia washed the eggs and put them on a linen cloth to dry. Then she took the flour from the cupboard. Sometimes this daily ritual held special significance. It was the day of homemade desserts. Mamma called us together, around the table. My sisters and I kneeled on the straw-bottomed chairs made by Pi del Bac, who came to stay with us for a week every year. He slept in the stall next to Rosalpina, our beloved cow, who gave us milk for breakfast, and butter. Mamma had learned from Grandma how to transform these products into happiness. With them she made lemon cream, chocolate pudding and a thousand kinds of pie, all different. And at Carnival time, sweet fritters and the "lattughe", that are known as "chiacchere" in Milan. It was fascinating to see her break the eggs with one blow against her wedding ring and then beat them, knead them with flour and roll out the dough. While outside, not far away, the war was raging..."

Crunchy cream-filled biscuits with Gianduia chocolate and black cherries in syrup

Ingredients

FOR THE BLACK CHERRIES
Pitted black cherries 1/2 cup
Sugar 2 1/2 teaspoons
Water 1/8 cup

FOR THE CRUNCHY BISCUITS
Honey 1 1/2 tablespoons
Butter 1/4 cup
Floor 1/2 cup
Sugar 2 tablespoons
Orange juice 1/8 cup

FOR THE SAUCE
Gianduia chocolate 2 1/2 oz
Water

FOR THE MOUSSE
Cream 1/2 cup
Zabaglione 1 tablespoon
(see recipe on page 218)
Sugar 1 tablespoon

Time: 1h
plus chilling time

Preparation

1. Simmer the black cherries in a small pot with the water and sugar for 10-15 minutes. You can then use the cherries at once or keep them in a closed jar.

2. For the crunchy biscuits, melt the butter with the honey in a small pan over very low heat; pour into a bowl with the sugar and stir to form a liquid batter. Then add the flour, stir gently and lastly add the orange juice.

3. Refrigerate the batter for 1 hour and then spread it onto Silpat (a silicone baking mat), forming rectangles about cm 3" x 2". Bake at 340 °F/170 °C for 7 minutes.
Let the biscuits cool for 1-2 minutes, then shape them with a cylindrical mould.

4. For the sauce, melt the Gianduia chocolate in a pan over hot water, adding a little water to form a sauce of the right density.

5. For the mousse, whip the cream with the sugar and then fold in the zabaglione. Refrigerate for 20 minutes before using.

6. Using a pastry bag, fill the crunchy biscuits with the mousse. Serve them with the black cherries in syrup and the Gianduia sauce.

In the glass: suggested wines

I capitelli – Anselmi (Veneto); Picolit Colli Orientali del Friuli – Livio Felluga (Friuli); Moscato d›Asti Vigna Senza Nome - Braida (Piemonte); Moscato Vendemmia Tardiva "le Rane" – Luretta (Lombardy); Riesling Grains Nobles – Trimbach (Alsace, France).

Meringue puffs with Bronte pistachio mousse and toasted almonds

Ingredients

FOR THE MOUSSE
Fresh cream 2/3 cup
Sugar 1/4 cup
Bronte pistachio paste 2 teaspoons

FOR THE MERINGUE PUFFS
Egg white 1
Powdered sugar 1/3 cup

Time: 1h20'
plus chilling time

Preparation

1. For the meringue, whip the egg whites until stiff, using a planetary mixer over water heated to a temperature of 150° F/70 °C, adding the sugar a little at a time. When the meringue has become very firm, place it in a pastry bag and squeeze it out in small puffs onto a wide pan covered with a sheet of oven paper. Cook the meringue puffs in a ventilated oven at 250° F/120 °C for 50-60 minutes.

2. For the mousse, delicately whip the cream with the sugar, adding the pistachio paste at the end. Stir gently to form a smooth, even mixture. Refrigerate for at least 20 minutes.

3. Using a pastry bag, arrange the mousse at the centre of a platter, surrounding it with the meringue puffs and the almonds, sliced fine and toasted.

This dessert can also be enriched with Marsala-flavoured zabaglione.

In the glass: suggested wines

Moscato naturale d'Asti – Rivetti (Piemonte); Moscato Rosa – Franz Haas (Alto Adige); Picolit Colli Orientali del Friuli – Livio Felluga (Friuli); Albana di Romagna Scaccomatto – Fattoria La Zerbina (Emilia Romagna).

Peach and cherry compote with berry tisane and Amalfi lemon sherbet

Ingredients

Nectarines 4
Cherries 12
Sugar 4 tablespoons
Water 2 cups
Dry white wine 1 1/4 cups
Lemon (juice of) 1/2
Dried berries for herbal teas 6 tablespoons
Amalfi lemon sherbet (optional)

Time: **1h**

Preparation

1. Heat the water, white wine, sugar and lemon juice in a pot over high heat.

2. Bring to boiling point, add the nectarines and the dried berries. Simmer for 4-5 minutes, depending on the size of the nectarines.

3. Remove the pot from the heat, add the cherries and let cool to room temperature.

4. Peel the nectarines, cut them in half to remove the stones and put them back into the pot.

5. Serve the nectarines in a deep dish with the cherries, the dried berries and if you wish, sherbet made of Amalfi lemons.

In summer we serve this compote cold.

In the glass: suggested wines

With this dessert we suggest a Moscato Rosa – F. Haas (Alto Adige); to accentuate the nectarine taste, you can also opt for a Bellini cocktail. Alternatively, we suggest: Vin Santo Pomino – Frescobaldi (Tuscany); Vin Santo – Avignonesi (Tuscany); Aestas Siciliae Moscato di Noto – Cos (Sicily). Another excellent wine is Pinot Gris Vendange Tardive – Dom. Zind Humbrecht (Alsace, France).

Orange-scented soufflé with passion fruit coulis

Ingredients

FOR THE CUSTARD
Milk 1 1/2 cups
Vanilla bean 1
Egg yolks 5
Sugar 2/3 cup
Flour 2 tablespoons
Butter 2 teaspoons

FOR THE SOUFFLÉ
Custard 4 tablespoons
Egg yolks 2
Oranges (grated rind of) 2
Grand Marnier 2 tablespoons
Egg whites 4
Powdered sugar 1 tablespoon
Butter for the pyrex dishes
Sugar for the pyrex dishes

FOR THE COULIS
Water 1 ladle
Passion fruit 4
Sugar

Time: 50'

Preparation

1. For the custard, boil the milk with the vanilla bean. In the meantime, beat the egg whites with the sugar until smooth and creamy, then add the flour. Pour the milk and the beaten egg whites into a pot and simmer over moderate heat until the custard begins to swells in peaks. Remove the pot from the heat and stir the unmelted butter into it. Pour the custard into a metal pan, after having greased it with a little butter to keep it from drying too much. Let cool and then refrigerate.

2. For the soufflé, mix together in an aluminium pan the egg yolks, custard, Grand Marnier and grated orange rind. Cook over hot water, stirring constantly to form a smooth, warm batter.
In the meantime, whip the 4 egg whites with the powdered sugar until smooth but not stiff. Fold the whipped egg whites delicately into the batter, mixing from top to bottom until perfectly smooth and even. Pour the batter into small pyrex pans with diameter of 4"-5", previously buttered and sprinkled with sugar. Protect the soufflés by wrapping the pyrex pans in a cylinder of buttered oven paper, warm them by setting them in a large pan of hot water for one minute and then bake in the oven at 350 °F/180 °C for 20 minutes.

3. For the coulis, warm the water, add the passion fruit and heat gradually to 100 °F/40 °C; strain through a fine strainer and, if necessary, add more sugar.

4. You can serve the soufflés with a passion fruit coulis, which you can pour into the centre of each soufflé, opening it delicately with the aid of a spoon.

A dessert with many variables and an infinite range of subtle flavours, not all of them easy to harmonise, which has always been the true test of every chef. The secret of success in this endeavour? Try and try again; only in this way will you finally achieve results to be proud of.

In the glass: suggested wines

This soufflé goes beautifully with an elegant wine or a more structured wine, but with a good degree of acidity. We suggest a Moscato d'Asti – Spinetta (Piemonte) or a Moscato d'Asti – Braida (Piemonte) or, in alternative, a Riesling Sélection de Grain Nobles – Kientzler (Alsace, France), on condition that it is a young wine. Another excellent accompaniment would be a Châteux Clos Haut-Peyraguey (Sauternes, France).

dal Pescatore
Santini

Ladyfingers with berries and Chantilly cream

Ingredients

FOR THE LADYFINGERS
Butter 1/4 cup
Powdered sugar 1/2 cup
Flour 00 2/3 cup
Egg whites 2
Chestnut (or millefiori) honey
1 tablespoon

FOR THE CHANTILLY CREAM
Fresh, pasteurised whipping cream
(35% fat) 1 1/3 cups
Granulated sugar 1/4 cup
Lemon (grated rind of,
optional) 1/4

Berries (blackberries, raspberries,
blueberries) 4 small baskets

Time: **50'**

Preparation

1. For the ladyfingers, soften the butter at room temperature; when it is soft, add the powdered sugar and mix delicately. Then add the egg whites, stirring to form a creamy batter.
Sift the flour and mix it into the batter to thicken it to the right consistency. Flavour it with a tablespoon of chestnut honey (optional).

2. Form disks of dough about 4" in diameter and place them on an oven tray covered with a sheet of oven paper. Bake at 320 °F/160° C for 8-9 minutes. As they cook, the ladyfingers will begin to brown at the edges, then gradually turn an even golden colour. At this point they are done. Check while cooking that your oven is not too hot and that the edges do not burn immediately.

3. For the Chantilly cream, whip the cream with the sugar and, if you like, flavour it with grated lemon rind.

4. Place the whipped cream in a small pastry bag and distribute it over the ladyfingers, garnishing with berries.

This dessert, slightly clownish in appearance, is simple and easy to make.

In the glass: suggested wines

With this dessert the optimum is a light, delicate, sweet white wine, such as Moscato d'Asti – Braida (Piemonte); but try it with more complex wines as well: Picolit – L. Felluga (Friuli Venezia Giulia); Albana di Romagna Scaccomatto – Fattoria La Zerbina (Emilia Romagna); Le Colombare – Pieropan (Veneto); Capichera Vendemmia Tardiva (Sardinia).

VALRHONA 70% CHOCOLATE PENGUIN WITH CANDIED FRUIT MOUSSE AND PISTACHIO CREAM

Ingredients (serves 3)

FOR THE CHOCOLATE TUILES
Valrhona 70% chocolate 3 1/2 oz

FOR THE CANDIED FRUIT MOUSSE
Whipping cream 1 1/4 cups
Sugar 1/4 cup
Candied fruit 2 oz
Acacia honey 1 tablespoon

FOR THE PISTACHIO CREAM
Whipping cream 1/2 cup
Sugar 1 tablespoon
Pistachio paste 1 tablespoon
Milk

Time: 35'
plus chilling time

Preparation

1. For the tuiles, melt the chocolate over hot water. Cut a sheet of oven paper into disks about 3" in diameter and spread them with a layer of chocolate (to make the tuiles you can also use moulds, either wavy or in whatever shape you prefer).
Refrigerate the disks of chocolate at 40 °F/4 °C for about 20 minutes, until the chocolate can be easily detached from the oven paper.

2. For the candied fruit mousse, whip the cream with the sugar in a deep round bowl. Add the finely chopped candied fruit and a tablespoon of acacia honey; mix well.

3. For the pistachio cream, whip the cream with the sugar in a deep round bowl; add the pistachio paste and mix well, adding a little milk if the mixture is too thick.

4. Arrange the chocolate tuiles filled with candied fruit mousse on a platter; decorate with the pistachio cream and serve.

A dessert that exalts chocolate to the highest degree, with a candied fruit mousse enriched by pistachio cream.

IN THE GLASS: SUGGESTED WINES

For this cold dessert the sommelier Mototsugu Hayashi has chosen classic meditation wines: Moscato di Noto – Planeta (Sicily); Moscato di Pantelleria – De Bartoli (Sicily); Trochenbeerenauslese Grand Cuvée – Kracher (Austria); Château Rieussec (Sauternes, France); Ron Zacapa Centenario Etiqueta Negra 23 años (Guatemala).

dal Pescatore
Santini

Crumbly biscuits with Amedei 75% chocolate ganache and mascarpone roll

Ingredients

FOR THE CRUMBLY BISCUITS
Flour 2 cups
Sugar 3/4 cup
Baker's ammonia 2 1/2 teaspoons
Orange (grated rind of) 1
Butter 1/2 cup
Strega liqueur 1 tablespoon
Rum 1 teaspoon
Whole eggs 2
Granulated sugar
Vanilla powder 1 packet

FOR THE CHOCOLATE GANACHE
Water 1 tablespoon
Milk 5 tablespoons
Amedei dark chocolate (75% cocoa butter) 2 2/3 oz
Cream 1/3 cup
Sugar 1 tablespoon

FOR THE MASCARPONE CREAM
Egg yolks 2
Sugar
Egg whites 1
Mascarpone 1/3 cup
Brandy 1 tablespoon

Rum
Powdered cocoa

Time: 1h20'
plus chilling time

Preparation

1. For the crumbly biscuits, soften the butter at room temperature in a deep, round bowl; add all of the other ingredients and mix well to form a smooth, creamy dough; if necessary, add a little milk.
Refrigerate the dough at 40 °F/4 °C for an hour. Then divide it in half and roll each half with a rolling pin to a thickness of about 1/8". Brush the dough with the egg white and sprinkle it with the granulated sugar.
Cut the biscuits in any shape you like and place them on a buttered oven pan. Bake at 350 °F/180 °C for 5-6 minutes.

2. For the chocolate ganache, heat the water and milk in a pan. Bring to the boiling point, then pour into a pitcher containing the dark chocolate broken into bits (the chocolate should be almost entirely immersed in the liquid). Set aside to rest for 2 minutes, then blend to form a rather liquid batter. In the meantime, whip the cream with the sugar in a deep round bowl. Add it to the liquid batter, mix well and refrigerate at 40 °F/4 °C for 2 hours.

3. For the mascarpone cream, whip the egg white until stiff. In another bowl, beat the egg yolks with the sugar and then delicately fold in the mascarpone. Add the brandy and fold in the whipped egg white, mixing from top to bottom; refrigerate at 35 °F/2° C.

4. You can also flavour your biscuits with a few drops of rum; spread them with the chocolate ganache, sprinkle with powdered cocoa and serve with the mascarpone cream.

In this dessert, the bitter note characteristic of the dark chocolate ganache melds sublimely with the creamy taste of mascarpone.

In the glass: suggested wines

With our crumbly biscuits, you can dare to try many different combinations. They go very well with the range of rums selected by Silvano Samaroli and imported by Giuseppe Mongiardino, two remarkable people who have dedicated their lives to choosing great products for the Italian market. Another excellent choice is Aleatico dell'Elba Capoliveri – Meletti Cavallari (Tuscany). To our own choices we add the precious advice of the sommelier Mototsugu Hayashi: Ben Ryé Passito di Pantelleria 2005 – Donnafugata (Sicily); Porto – Vintage Graham's (Portugal); Vin Santo San Giusto – Fattoria San Giusto a Rentennano (Tuscany); Marsala Vergine Baglio Florio 1993 – Florio (Sicily).

Baba au rhum

Ingredients (serves 6-8)

Sifted flour 3 cups
Yeast 1/2 tablespoon
Warm milk 8 tablespoons
Eggs 4
Sugar 1 tablespoon
Salt 1/2 teaspoon
Softened butter 2/3 cup

FOR THE SYRUP
Water 4 1/2 ladles
Sugar 1 cup
Top quality rum 12 tablespoons

Apricot jam 1/3 cup
Vanilla ice cream

Time: **2h**

Preparation

1. For the baba, put the flour in a bowl, add the yeast after having dissolved it in warm milk and then the lightly beaten eggs. Work with the hands to form a rather sticky dough; drop the ball of dough several times onto the bottom of the bowl.
Cover the dough with a fine cloth and let it rise in a warm place until it has doubled in volume (about one hour).
Place the dough on a lightly floured wooden board, flatten and spread it with your hands, sprinkle it with salt and sugar, and then spread the softened butter on it with your hands. Knead it again for 2-3 minutes, lifting it and letting it fall to the bottom of the bowl.
Butter pastry moulds and fill them half full of the dough; put the moulds in a warm place until the dough has risen again enough to fill them to the top. Bake at 320 °F/160 °C for 15-20 minutes. When the cakes have turned golden brown, remove them from the oven and turn them out of the moulds.

2. Meanwhile, to make the rum syrup, mix the water with the sugar in a pan. Bring to the boil and cook for 6 minutes. Remove from the heat and add 12 tablespoons of the finest rum. Let cool.

3. Soak the cakes in the cold syrup and serve them accompanied by vanilla ice cream or apricot jam diluted in a little water and passed through a sieve.

A classic recipe of Neapolitan pastry tradition, a delicious dessert that we recommend enhancing with a noble rum, to add a refined note to your own version of it.

In the glass: suggested wines

In my opinion, the ideal accompaniment would be the same rum used for the syrup, which should be of top quality. On the Italian market you can find an extraordinary range of rums: from Jamaica, Ecuador, Haiti, Cuba and various other countries. You only have to try the different types and different ages.

dal Pescatore

Vanilla-flavoured pineapple macaroni with apricots, peppermint and blended raspberries

Ingredients

FOR THE FILLING
Cream 1/3 cup
Sugar 1 tablespoon
Vanilla extract 1 teaspoon

Pineapple 1/3
Mint 20 small leaves
Apricots 2
Raspberries 1 small basket

FOR THE THREADS OF CARAMELISED SUGAR
Sugar 1 heaping tablespoon

Time: **20'**

Preparation

1. For the filling, blend the cream with the sugar until firm, then add the vanilla extract.

2. Cut the pineapple in slices with a maximum thickness of 1/8". Roll each slice to form a cylinder; cut each cylinder in half.

3. Arrange the cylinders vertically on a serving platter, one beside another, to form a circle of 6 little "chimneys".

4. For the caramelised sugar, dissolve 2 tablespoons of sugar over moderate heat until it turns amber yellow; then with the aid of a knife, form a thread of sugar that will solidify immediately.

5. Using a pastry bag, fill the pineapple cylinders with the vanilla-flavoured cream and decorate with wedges of apricot. Add small mint leaves for more flavour and, if you wish, garnish with threads of caramelised sugar.
Serve accompanied by the blended raspberries.

A summer dessert, light and pleasantly fresh.

In the glass: suggested wines

Our sommelier Mototsugu Hayashi suggests for this dessert: Moscato d'Asti 2007 – La Spinetta (Piemonte); Muffato della Sala 2005 – Castello della Sala (Umbria); Aureus Passito 2004 – Niedermayr (Alto Adige); Picolit 2003 – Le Vigne di Zamò (Friuli Venezia Giulia).

75% DARK CHOCOLATE CAKE

Ingredients

Dark chocolate (75% cocoa butter) 3 1/2 oz
Whole eggs 2
Butter 3 tablespoons
Flour 1 heaping tablespoon
Sugar 1/4 cup

FOR THE CHOCOLATE FROSTING
Dark chocolate 1 oz
Water

Apricot jam

Time: **50'**

Preparation

1. Whip the sugar with the egg yolks.

2. In the meantime, melt the chocolate over hot water, add the unmelted butter and mix well.

3. Combine the two mixtures, stir well and incorporate the flour.

4. In a separate bowl, whip the egg whites until stiff and fold them into the chocolate batter. Fold in delicately, stirring from top to bottom to keep the batter light and smooth.

5. Pour the batter into a cake pan; bake at 345 °F/175 °C for 30 minutes. When the cake is done, remove it from the oven and let it cool.

6. For the chocolate frosting, melt the chocolate over hot water. Add the water a little at a time, stirring until creamy.

7. Cut the cake horizontally into two halves, spread the lower half with apricot jam, cover with the other half and glaze with the chocolate frosting.

Chocolate cake is a classic of pastry-making that transports us to the fantastic world of culinary delight.

IN THE GLASS: SUGGESTED WINES

With this cake we suggest: Aleatico dell'Elba Capoliveri – Meletti Cavallari (Tuscany); Recioto della Valpolicella – G. Allegrini (Veneto); Recioto della Valpolicella – Quintarelli (Veneto); Recioto della Valpolicella Le Pergole Vecie – Le Salette (Veneto); Porto Vintage 1967 – Croft (Portugal); Porto Vintage 1970 – Sandeman (Portugal).

dal Pescatore

White cake

Ingredients

Eggs 12
Potato starch 1 1/2 cups
Sugar 1 1/4 cups
Vanilla powder 3 packets
Baking powder 1 packet
Lemons (juice of) 2
Liqueur (optional) 2 tablespoons

FOR THE ZABAGLIONE
Egg yolks 5
Sugar 1/3 cup
Dry Marsala 3 tablespoons
Dry white wine 3 tablespoons

Butter

Time: **1h**

Preparation

1. Whip the egg whites until stiff.

2. Mix the egg yolks and sugar, stirring to form a creamy batter.

3. Fold in the stiffly whipped egg whites; then add the sieved potato starch, the vanilla, baking powder and lemon juice. At your discretion, you can flavour the cake with 2 tablespoons of liqueur.

4. Butter a cake pan and pour the batter into it.

5. Put the cake in the oven preheated to the temperature of 120-140 °F/50-60 °C; then raise the temperature to 350 °F/180 °C and bake for 30 minutes; cooking slowly, the cake will be soft and fluffy (check for doneness by inserting a long needle; when it comes out dry, the cake is done).

6. For the zabaglione, beat the egg yolks and sugar with a wire whisk to form a soft, straw-yellow cream. Continue to whip, adding a little at a time the white wine and dry Marsala. Cook the zabaglione over hot water for 10 minutes, stirring constantly. It will be perfectly done when it starts to become very firm around the edges of the pan.

7. Remove the cake from the oven, let it cool and serve it with the warm zabaglione.

In Mantua, this truly simple cake has always been cooked by mothers and grandmothers to celebrate the birthdays of young children.

IN THE GLASS: SUGGESTED WINES

With this delicate dessert we advise an elegant wine. Our choice falls once again on Moscato d'Asti, absolutely perfect: Moscato d'Asti – La Morandina (Piemonte); Moscato d'Asti Forteto della Luja – Scaglione (Piemonte).

Tagliatelle pie

Ingredients

Tagliatelle dough 1/3 lb
Sweetened pie dough 2/3 lb
Ladyfinger dough (see recipe on page 206) 1/3 lb

FOR THE TAGLIATELLE
Flour 4 cups
Egg yolks 7
Egg whites 3-4

FOR THE SWEETENED PIE DOUGH
Flour 4 cups
Butter 1 cup
Sugar 1 1/4 cups
Egg yolks 5
Marsala or Port 1 tablespoon
Orange (grated rind of) 1
Salt 1 pinch

Apples 1/3 cup
Finely sliced almonds 1/3 cup
Chopped pistachio nuts 2 1/2 tablespoons
Crumbled amaretti 3 tablespoons
Powdered sugar 1 tablespoons
Green lemon (rind of)
Orange (rind of)

Zabaglione cream
Vanilla ice cream

Time: 25'
plus chilling time

Preparation

1. For the tagliatelle dough, work all of the ingredients together and, if necessary, add another 1/3 cup of flour. Roll the dough very fine and let it dry for 5 minutes; then roll it onto itself and cut it in very fine strips, forming little nests.

2. For the pie dough, mix all of the ingredients together in a bowl and work well to form a dough. Refrigerate the dough for at least an hour, then roll it to form a disk, place it on an oven tray and prick with a fork. Bake at 340 °F/170 °C for 10 minutes.

3. When the pie dough has browned a little, remove it from the oven and cover it with the ladyfinger dough, then arrange on it the nests of tagliatelle (you can move the nests around without fear of breaking them, since the dough, although cut very fine, is elastic).

4. Garnish with the almonds, pistachios, amaretti, green lemon rind and the orange rind cut into small pieces.

5. Put the pie back into the oven and bake at 340 °F/170 °C until the tagliatelle are glossy and golden brown.

6. Sprinkle the pie with powdered sugar. Serve it hot in winter with the zabaglione cream, cold in summer with vanilla ice cream.

The tagliatelle dough, unexpectedly appearing here in the recipe for a dessert, is the same used to make tortelli and fettuccine. The secret of the golden yellow colour is the fact that egg yolks are one of the main ingredients; the elasticity of the pasta, instead, results from the presence of egg whites.

In the glass: suggested wines

Le Rane – Luretta (Emilia Romagna); Ben Ryé Moscato Passito – Donnafugata (Sicily); Muscat du Cap Corse – Dom. Gentile (Corsica, France); Vin Santo – Castellare (Tuscany); Château Climens – Barsac (France); I Capitelli – R. Anselmi (Veneto).

Reinette apple strudel with apricot and peach jam

Ingredients

FOR THE STRUDEL DOUGH
Flour 1 1/4 cups
Butter 1/2 cup
Water or milk (warm) 2 tablespoons
Whole eggs 1
Pinch of salt 1
Breadcrumbs 1/3 cup

FOR THE FILLING
Reinette apples 4-6
Butter 3 tablespoons
Sugar 1/4 cup
Apricot and peach jam
Rinds of orange and green lemon
Cloves (optional)
Cinnamon (optional)

FOR THE JAM
Fruit as desired, in proportion to the sugar
Sugar 3 cups for every 2 1/4 lbs of fruit

Granulated sugar 2 tablespoons

Time: 1h40'
plus cooling of the jam

Preparation

1. For the strudel dough, work together all of the ingredients except the bread crumbs, shape the dough into a ball and beat it against a breadboard for 6-7 minutes, to soften it. Put the dough in a bowl, cover it with a cloth and keep it warm for 30 minutes.

2. For the filling, peel 4-6 Reinette apples, cut them into large pieces and sauté them in a pan with the sugar and butter; add the orange and green lemon rind and, if you like, cloves and cinnamon. When the apples have become caramelised (4-5 minutes), remove them from the pan and set aside.

3. On a lightly floured cotton cloth, roll the dough with a rolling pin to a thickness of 1/16".

4. Heat 2 tablespoons di butter mixed with 2 tablespoons of breadcrumbs. Spread this mixture over the dough, to absorb the excess juice from the fruit. Cover the dough with apricot and peach jam, and with the caramelised apples. With the aid of the cotton cloth, roll the strudel up.

5. Place the strudel on an oven tray, brush it with a little egg yolk and garnish it with the granulated sugar.

6. Bake at 350 °F/175 °C until golden brown.

7. For the jam, wash the fruit and cut it in half to remove the stones. Weigh it and put it in a large pot. Then add the sugar, cover with a sheet of oven paper and set aside to rest for 24 hours. Cook the jam in a deep pot, stirring constantly with a wooden spatula to keep it from sticking. When the spatula becomes coated, the jam is done (about 30 minutes). If you intend to store it, use very hot glass jars with screw tops; fill them with the jam and close the tops immediately. Turn the jars upside down and leave them to cool; the vacuum that forms in this way will ensure perfect preservation.

This classic of Austrian pastry-making is very popular throughout Northeastern Italy.

In the glass: suggested wines

Le Pergole del Sole – Cavalchina (Veneto); Albana di Romagna Scaccomatto – Zerbina (Emilia Romagna); Muscat du Cap Corse – Dom. Gentile (Corsica, France); Trochenbeeren Auslese Grand Cuvée – Kracher (Austria).

Fox grape sherbet

Ingredients

Fox grapes 1 3/4 lbs
Sugar 20-25% of the weight of the blended grapes
Water

Time: $1^{h}15'$

Preparation

1. Wash the grapes, carefully detach the stems and put them in the blender. Blend well, then strain.

2. In a stainless steel pot, heat the blended grapes to the boiling point. With a skimmer, remove the foam that forms on the surface. Simmer for about 10 minutes to entirely eliminate the impurities present in the foam, then set aside to cool.

3. Weigh the grape mixture and calculate the amount of sugar to be added for the sherbet as 20-25 percent of its weight.

4. Heat some water in a pan and dissolve the sugar in it.

5. Add the water and sugar mixture to the blended grapes and pour into an ice-cream machine.

6. When the sherbet is ready, you can either serve it immediately or keep it in the freezer.

The same procedure can be followed in recipes for other kinds of fruit. The amount of sugar, usually 20-30 percent of the weight of the blended fruit, is fundamental for the creaminess of the sherbet; the more the sugar, the creamier it will be. A lower sugar content, instead, will make the micro-crystals in the sherbet more perceptible to the taste.

dal Pescatore
Santini

Peach or apricot gelatine

Ingredients

Peaches, quantity in proportion to the sugar
Apricots, quantity in proportion to the sugar
Sugar 1/2 cup + 1 tablespoon for every 1/2 cup of blended fruit

Time: **1h**

Preparation

1. Choose ripe, tasty fruit. Wash and dry it without peeling it, then cut each piece in half to remove the stones. Put the fruit in a large pan.

2. Add enough water to cover the fruit and simmer over moderate heat until the water has evaporated but the fruit has not become mushy.

3. Strain the cooked fruit through a very fine strainer, crushing it well to press all of the pectin out of the skins. Weigh the strained fruit, put it back in the pan and cover it with the sugar.

4. Simmer over low heat, stirring constantly with a wooden palette until the mixture begins to detach from the sides of the pan and becomes as thick as boiled custard. If you have a cooking thermometer, you can control the cooking more easily; continuing to stir, remove the gelatine from the heat when it reaches the temperature of around 220 °F/105 °C.

5. Pour the gelatine into a mould or a pan lined with oven paper, to form a layer about 3/4" thick.

6. Shape small portions of gelatine as desired; roll them in sugar (optional) and serve them.

An idea for these friandises: tasty delights that satisfy children's craving for sweets in an entirely natural manner.

In the glass: suggested wines

These delicious sweets are so delicate that they need no wine to accompany them; but if you wish, a light Moscato d'Asti will go well with them.

Rosolio, nocino, limoncello ("Grandma Bruna's three liqueurs")

Ingredients

ROSOLIO
Roses (use highly perfumed, untreated roses) 100 petals
95° alcohol 1 quart
Water 1 quart
Sugar 4 cups

NOCINO
Green walnuts (picked on St. John's day, in June) 40
95° alcohol 5 1/4 quarts
Water 5 1/4 quarts
Sugar 7 3/4 lbs

LIMONCELLO
Lemons 12
95° alcohol 1 quart
Sugar 5 cups
Water 1 quart

Preparation

Rosolio

1. Put the rose petals in a 1-quart jar and add the alcohol; set aside to rest for 1-2 days.

2. Heat the water mixed with the sugar to the boiling point, then let it cool and add it to the rose petals in alcohol. Set the liqueur aside to rest for one month.

Nocino

1. Cut the walnuts in half and place them in a 5-quart jar together with the alcohol.

2. After 3-4 days, boil the sugar with the water. Let the mixture cool, then add it to the jar with the walnuts in alcohol.

3. Set the Nocino aside to rest for at least 40 days, to let it age and improve the flavour.

Limoncello

1. To make this liqueur, use only thin lemon rinds, without the white part. Place them in a 1-quart jar and add the alcohol. Set aside to rest for one month.

2. After 30 days, boil the water with the sugar. Let it cool and then add it to the lemon rind and alcohol mixture.

An anecdote on the subject of Nocino: Renzi di Modena, a great master in the construction of casks for balsamic vinegar, and our supplier, once let me taste the Nocino he makes, aged in the casks he produces. After having tasted it, I decided to follow him in this adventure, and ordered three oaken casks. Applying the system of moving the liqueur from larger to smaller casks, I decided to age my Nocino. After seven years, I tasted it: the results were truly excellent. This liqueur, an integral part of the Modena culinary tradition, is also common to the whole eastern Po Valley, from Ferrara to Mantua, from Cremona to Parma, and as far as Reggio Emilia.

Collection of menus from the restaurant Dal Pescatore (above, from left): 2013 G. Frangi; 2011 F. Di Piazza; 2008 F. Scalvini; 2007 G. Busnago; 2006 A. Parmigiani; 2005 M. Ashkhotov; 2003 M. Ashkhotov; 2001 A. Parmigiani; 1999 A. Dal Prato; 1998 A. Fusco; 1995 F. Scalvini; 1992 F. Scalvini; 1988 A. De Benedetti; 1980 Milzani; 1974 Milzani; 1996 C. Cressini.

dal Pescatore
Santini

Alphabetical index of recipes

Credits

Archivio Giunti / Francesca Brambilla e Serena Serrani:
pp. 2-3, 4, 6, 9, 10, 12, 16-25, 28-29, 35r, 39, 43, 46-49, 56-57, 66-69, 104-105, 107, 144-145, 147, 194-195, 197, 230-31, 234, 237, 238-39 and all the still-lifes of the recipes

© Maurice Rougemont
pp. 31, 35, 36, 37 l/c, 40, 41, 50 al/bl, 52d

© Philippe Schaff
pp. 26, 36-37, 50ar, 51r, 52s, 53/146 (part.), 55, 63, 64-65, 106

© Sandro Vannini / Corbis
pp. 58ar, 60 (part.)

© Della Zuana Pascal / Corbis Sygma
pp. 58bl, 62 (part.)

We would like to thank the restaurant *Auberge de l'ill* own by Marc Haeberlin, and particulary Ms Sophie, to have granted us the use of the images at pages 58br and p. 61 (part.)

Giovanni
dal